WORDS

— TO —

LOVE BY

Elemental Building Blocks of a
"Wildly Successful Marriage"

KIMBERLY & JOEL WALTON

Copyright © 2022

Words to Love By Book
7844 Madison Ave
Suite 108
Fair Oaks, CA 95628
www.WordstoLoveByBook.com

Ordering Information:
For details, contact Info@WordstoLoveByBook.com.

Cover design   Klassic Designs – 99Designs.com
Interior layout   Olivier Darbonville – www.darbonville.com
Distribution   Bookbaby – 7905 N. Crescent Blvd. Pennsauken, NJ 09110

Print ISBN: 978-1-66783-554-9
eBook ISBN: 978-1-66783-555-6

Printed in the United States of America on SFI Certified paper.

First Edition

DEDICATION

———

We'd like to dedicate this book to all the individuals and couples we've had the honor and privilege to come alongside and work with over the thousands of hours of coaching and counseling. Thank you for letting us be a part of your journey as you created your own **"Wildly Successful Marriage."**

ACKNOWLEDGEMENTS

———

Special thanks to: **Ashley, Andrea, and Kassandra**.

Ashley, for the depth of suggestions, feedback, and editing. You kept us moving, Ashley, and we couldn't have completed the book without you. Thanks for being our muse, our writing angel, and for the relentless support.

Andrea, for the thorough editing. Thank you for believing in this project and dedicating your time to help us get it to the final stages.

Kassandra, for the initial chapter reads and thoughtful feedback as well as the enduring encouragement and unwavering belief in the ideas in the book.

And a special thanks to our friends and family who supported this project and for their never-ending patience and understanding when we had to postpone gatherings, rearrange coffee and lunch dates, and had to opt out of activities to meet writing deadlines to complete this project.

NOTICES

[All names and events depicted throughout this book are made up in whole or in part.]

[This book is for educational purposes only and shouldn't be viewed as a substitute for professional counseling.]

CONTENTS

How to Use This Book   11
Information on the different ways to read this book

Introduction   13
Why the world needs another book on relationships

Building Your Tower of Love   21
The ABCs of a "Wildly Successful Marriage"

WORDS TO LOVE BY

A = Awareness / ə-ˈwer-nəs /   28
A well-informed interest; the ability to know and perceive, to feel, or to be cognizant of something or someone.

B = Beliefs / bə-ˈlēf /   35
Trust, faith, or confidence in something or someone.

C = Conflict / kän-ˌflikt /   46
The tension that is created between two opposing needs, wants, or desires within a relationship.

D = Desire / di-ˈzī(-ə)r /   55
The emotion of longing or hoping for a person, object, or outcome.

E = Engagement / in-ˈgāj-mənt /   63
Taking action to maintain or improve one's relationship with another.

F = Flexibility / flek-sə-bəl /   71

An openness to consider or reconsider another person's view, in whole or in part, before insisting that your own view is the best course of action.

G = Gratitude / gra-tə-ˌtüd /   79

The quality or feeling of being grateful or thankful.

H = Hope / hōp /   88

A desire accompanied by an expectation or belief that it will be fulfilled.

I = Intimacy / in-tə-mə-sē /   96

The emotional and spiritual union between two people.

J = Joining / jȯi-niŋ /   105

Coming together; becoming a cohesive unit; working collaboratively and collectively.

K = Knowledge / nä-lij /   113

An awareness or familiarity of yourself and your mate gained by experience.

L = Loyalty / lȯi(-ə)l-tē /   123

A strong feeling of support, devotion, or allegiance.

M = Mending / mend-ing /   130

To repair something that is broken or damaged; to return to health; to heal.

N = Novelty / nä-vəl-tē /   141

The quality of being new, original, unique, or unusual.

O = Opportunity / ä-pər-ˈtü-nə-tē /   150

Circumstances that make it possible to know, serve, support, and grow with your mate; a moment, time, or chance to be used wisely.

P = Protect / prə-ˈtekt /   160
To cover or shield from exposure, injury, damage, or
destruction; to maintain the integrity of; to guard.

Q = Quieting / kwī-ət-ing /   171
To silence, still, and calm; to make less noisy, less active,
or less busy.

R = Regulation / re-gyə-ˈlā-shən /   179
One's ability to interact and stay emotionally and logically
connected with themselves and others during times of fear,
stress, and conflict.

S = Safety / sāf-tē /   189
Freedom from danger, risk, or injury.

T = Trust / trəst /   197
The confidence that one is true and authentic and can be
depended on to carry out what they've stated they will or will
not do.

U = Understanding / ən-dər-ˈstan-diŋ /   206
A perception and knowledge of the significance, cause, character,
and nature of something.

V = Vulnerability / vəl-n(ə-)rə-bəl /   214
Uncertainty, risk, and susceptibility; the quality or state of
emotional exposure.

W = Wise-Counsel / wīz – kȧun(t)-səl /   222
Getting the best advice. Only the wise can give it and only the
wise will listen and receive it.

X = X-Factor / X – fak-tər /   232
The willingness and desire to have an active form of physical
intimacy between you and your partner.

Y = Yea-sayer / yā-ˌsā-ər /   240

One who has an attitude of confident affirmation, belief in,
and support.

Z = Zebraesque / zē-brə-esk /   248

No two zebras have the same stripes, and no two marriages
are exactly the same. Be wildly different.

SUMMARY

Final Thoughts   257

Things to consider as you build your own "Wildly Successful Marriage"

About the Authors   261

Kimberly & Joel Walton

HOW TO USE
THIS BOOK

—

THIS BOOK IS DESIGNED TO BE USED AS AN INDIVIDUAL, A COUPLE, or a small group. You can approach the book alphabetically, reading it from cover to cover in just a few hours, or you can slow it down by delving into just one chapter per week. Perhaps your style is to skip to the chapters you're most interested in. You can also take the categorical approach we've described below. Any way you choose to read this book is acceptable.

Understandably, different chapters will speak more to some people than others. Some may not seem that important now but will mean more later. We suggest, however, that the chapters on Awareness, Conflict, and Regulation are great places to begin if you are like most couples we've gotten to know in our practices.

Each of the 26 chapters (which we call "elements") is roughly 2,500 words, and each chapter includes questions at the end ("A Look in The Mirror") for further thought and discussion. If you are using this book as a small group or in premarital counseling, please reach out to us at https://www.WordsToLoveByBook.com for additional resources. We're happy to help!

For best results, we encourage you to complete the questions at the end of each chapter. We also want to stress that elements should not be treated with a "one-and-done" approach. Instead, as you go through life changes and seasons, you'll find yourself rereading some chapters and seeing others as more relevant than before.

To help you search with specific goals in mind, we broke down all the elements into seven categories. Below is a brief explanation of each category in case you find it useful.

THE SEVEN CATEGORIES AND THEIR ASSOCIATED ELEMENTS

Attunement
Awareness - Beliefs - Knowledge - Understanding

Resiliency
Conflict - Mending - Wise Counsel

Optimism
Gratitude - Hope - Opportunity - Protect

Connection
Desire - Intimacy - Vulnerability - X-Factor

Discerning
Flexibility - Quieting - Regulation - Safety

Commitment
Engagement - Joining - Loyalty - Trust

Originality
Novelty - Yea-sayer - Zebraesque

INTRODUCTION

—

D ID YOU KNOW THAT THE MOVIE TITANIC WAS ONE OF THE HIGHEST grossing films of all time?

Although the storyline has little to do with the actual historic events of the ill-fated ship, people rushed to see it and even saw it a second or third time. Why? Because we fell in love with the love story. We were drawn into the passion of Jack and Rose, their unity against the common foe of Rose's fiancé Cal (and maybe even her mother, Ruth!) and the life-and-death struggle of trying to survive a sinking ship. As the Celine Dion song goes, *My Heart Will Go On.*

But did you ever ask yourself what would have happened if Jack and Rose were a real couple and Rose had made room for Jack on the door? (And yes, there was room on that door for sure!)

If Jack had lived, how would their love story have played out?

People love a passionate romance, but we can't help but wonder—honestly—how Jack and Rose would have tackled real-life situations like Rose's overbearing and class-conscious mother, a special needs child, an attraction to a coworker, the loss of a job, health issues, mid-life crisis, addictions … we could go on. (Like the heart, we can go on and on.)

Okay, without ruining the story completely, would they have been one of the often-cited 50% of marriages that fail?

Consider the passionate, albeit fictitious, relationship of Noah and Allie from the blockbuster movie, *The Notebook,* adapted from the best-selling Nicolas Sparks book. Unlike Jack and Rose, we get a glimpse of Noah and Allie's life together. Spoiler alert—we get to see them growing old and learn that they had children and faced health challenges. What we don't get to see are challenges and brutal arguments related to differences in child rearing, infertility struggles, money problems, dealing with a meddling mother-in-law and ex-lovers, potential physical abuse, and so much more. So, we are left with the idea that it all went smoothly after the initial rough patch. Working in the business of relationships, we are securely confident that this relationship would have had many rough patches. (Note that he does keep the "in sickness and in health" vow, though!)

Think of your favorite fairy tale, maybe *Cinderella, Snow White and the Seven Dwarfs, Rapunzel, Sleeping Beauty,* or *Beauty and the Beast.* We are left to assume that all is well and life runs smoothly as they ride off into the sunset and their "happily ever after". But what if we found out that Rapunzel has debilitating migraine headaches due to her hair, and Snow White has food allergies that make meal planning a constant frustration and eating out impossible for her and her prince? What if Sleeping Beauty has narcolepsy and cannot drive or work, and Belle loves her Beast but considers him uncouth and often feels embarrassed by his lack of refinement?

> Relationships are about more than love and passion. They are about growing, learning, attuning, joining, adapting, and more.

This doesn't mean that their marriages can't be happy and fulfilling. No, it just means that like real life couples, they have challenges that need to be addressed and overcome.

Relationships are about more than love and passion. They are about growing, learning, attuning, joining, adapting, and more.

Sure—some couples make it look easy. For many of those couples, what you don't see is the behind-the-scenes work and difficult conversations (we are big on difficult conversations to avoid difficult situations), miscommunications, close calls, the contemplative thoughts, hurt feelings, frustrations, and even growth. These are all part of the journey. They are not to be feared, but rather can be understood, expected, embraced, and overcome.

Why We Wrote This Book

When we first pondered writing this book, we asked ourselves, "Does the world really need another relationship book?" Based on the divorce rates and how full our counseling practices are, we would have to say a resounding "Yes!"

We approached this project by making a list of the common areas that we see couples repeatedly struggling with, topics and troubles that we found were almost universal (but uniquely experienced by each couple).

We pushed the project to the back burner repeatedly and pulled it back off time and again. Every time the project got pushed to the back burner, something would come up in real life that made us wish we had this book to share with this or that client or small group. The repeated nudges telling us that this book was needed never ceased.

We know three things about troubled relationships: 1) Most can be saved. 2) People often have regrets after divorce, and 3) Most couples wait too long to begin counseling.

If you are reading this and are in a troubled relationship, know that we firmly believe that most troubled marriages can indeed be saved. No, not all, but many can if both parties are willing to do the work. And when the work is done, wisdom comes. In fact, when the work and effort are put in, the relationship can be stronger than ever before, even after betrayals.

Wisdom can carry you through future conflicts and disagreements, and yes, even healthy marriages have them. Behind that picture-perfect relationship the neighbors have is a lot of willingness to work through the universal challenges described in this book.

Working to save a difficult marriage is worth it. It is often easier to save a troubled marriage than end it and start a new relationship. And people often regret that they didn't try harder to work on their marriages once the fantasy of the grass being greener on the other side wears off. If you work to save your marriage and it does end in divorce, you will not look back and wonder if you gave up too soon. You will avoid the questions and lingering regrets that can leave you tethered to an ex.

It is never too early to strengthen and fortify a relationship and to learn new skills. Your marriage doesn't need to be in trouble for you to see that you can always use more information. Here's a list of common concerns we've worked to address in the pages of this book.

Common Issues and Concerns of Couples

1 **Do you feel as if your partner doesn't understand you?**
This is by far the most common complaint we hear when people come into the office. Do you feel your partner would react totally differently to you if only they understood you better?

2 **Do you feel you are stuck and that you've tried everything to fix your relationship?**
This is probably the second most common concern, and given enough time, will often lead to people making poor choices in an attempt to move past the logjam they are feeling.

3 **Do you feel there is a significant power imbalance between the two of you?**
Who has the power in your relationship, and in what areas? Do you feel you're limited or cut off in discussing details of life decisions in your relationship and family?

4 **Do you feel you can't be honest with your partner about your true feelings?**

If you share what you're really feeling, do you feel you'll be told you're wrong, judged, or rejected in some way? It's really hard to be authentic if you feel you'll be rejected.

5 **Do you feel you can't fully trust your partner with your heart?**

Are there things you've shared with your partner that they've shared with others, or they've later thrown back in your face? This often leads to broken trust between the two of you.

6 **Do you feel that you or your partner find little joy in serving each other?**

Mutual service between mates is an important part of a relationship. People want to feel a joy in serving as well as being served by their partner. When this is missing, things feel like a chore rather than a way to say, "I love seeing you happy."

7 **Do you get more fulfilment from kids, work, or other interests than your partner?**

People will often say they get more meaning and fulfillment from other areas of their life than their partner and that their relationship is more a utility of life than a source of inspiration and safety.

8 **Do you feel that if only you'd married the right person your marriage wouldn't be struggling so much?**

It's common to look at our problems and believe, "If only I'd married somebody else, I wouldn't have these problems." This is why too many people start to look up old partners on social media.

9 **Do you or your partner struggle to talk about aspects of your physical intimacy?**

One of the best indicators of how well a couple is communicating is how well they can talk about their intimacy differences in the bedroom. It's extremely common for spouses to have different wants, needs, and desires from one another. The question is, how easy is it for you to talk about them?

10 **Are you considering leaving your relationship?**

At times, we all think about what life would be like if we ended things, but are you honestly considering leaving your relationship? Are you currently working on an exit strategy?

11 **Are you struggling with family dynamics such as a blended family or in-law issues?**

Do you feel you are second, third, or even fourth in line in your partner's priorities? Are there significant loyalty issues between the two of you when it comes to feeling supported?

12 **Are you or your partner struggling with addictions or any repeated breach of trust?**

Humans are wired for relationships. When we struggle with addictions, we're attempting to have a pathological relationship with something that can't love us back. Building a strong relationship can go a long way in reducing those repeated negative patterns.

If you answer yes to or can relate to any of these 12 points, then this book is for you. You will find wisdom and strategies throughout the book to help you understand and address these most common concerns.

We hope that you enjoy this book as much as we enjoyed writing it. It's our life's work to help couples navigate the many twists and turns

> If you do find yourself in need of therapy, please don't feel shy about getting the help you need. It can change your life.

that life presents. While each individual and each couple is complex and unique, we put our hearts and souls into finding the most succinct and targeted messages to help the most number of people.

If you do find yourself in need of therapy, please don't feel shy about getting the help you need. It can change your life.

And please feel free to reach out to us and share your experience in reading this book. May your love grow and thrive as you navigate the seasons of your relationships.

Kimberly & Joel Walton

_Wise couples know
enough to work at
building and stabilizing
rather than waiting and
working on reassembly
and repair. They work to
build love rather than
seeking to find it._

BUILDING YOUR TOWER OF LOVE

—

The ABCs of a "Wildly Successful Marriage!"

Y OU'VE PROBABLY HEARD THE PHRASE, "WORDS TO LIVE BY". IT'S OF-
ten used to acknowledge the wisdom of a motto, pearl of wisdom, or quote that can serve as a guiding life principle.

Such as…

> *"You can't solve your problems with the same thinking that created them." —Albert Einstein*

> *"If you really want to do something, you'll find a way. If you don't, you'll find an excuse." —Jim Rohn*

> *"No one can make you feel inferior without your consent." —Eleanor Roosevelt*

> *"You don't love someone because they're perfect; you love them in spite of the fact that they're not." —Jodi Picoult*

We love these quotes and sayings. They're inspirational and can be valuable building blocks to a happier and more fulfilling life. They're literally "words to live by".

Through our years of working with clients in our counseling practices, we've come to realize that there are also what we call "Words to *Love* By"—words that are not just catchy phrases or mottos for life, but words of wisdom that represent the most important concepts couples need to learn in order to "love by".

Explaining Our Lexicon of Love

This book represents an A-to-Z lexicon of "words to love by" that we consistently find missing or underutilized in relationships, especially struggling marriages. These are words (or elements) not just to know and understand as concepts, but also to recognize the way they interconnect with the other elements of a strong relationship. The impact and output of these elements is what we have coined as the "Wildly Successful Marriage!"

The "Wildly Successful Marriage" is not meant to describe a relationship devoid of problems and challenges, but rather to describe a state of living and loving that's able to effectively navigate troubled waters and tough seasons in a couple's life. Wildly successful marriages are relationships that offer safe harbor for both individuals to attune, relate, and grow together (not apart), especially during those tough times.

True Love is Not Found—It's Built.

We are confident that you are familiar with the popular tumbling block games. In all areas of life, you have the power to create, build, and restore; or to destroy and dismantle. Wildly successful marriages are built from the ground up, much like what you do when you build your tower to start the game. *Words to Love By* is about building, fortifying, or reassembling your customized "tower of love" using a unique lexicon and internalizing the value of each word or element.

Love, like the game structure, will destabilize (or worse, tumble) if too many elements of the "tower" are removed, dislodged, or were never present in the first place. Without a good foundation, a relationship can be rocky from the beginning. Our lexicon of love can not only help you recognize weaknesses in your tower but can help you stabilize and add the missing elements.

Who wants to have a tower prone to collapse from the gentlest bump or a strong breeze? And who wants to self-sacrifice to preserve a fragile, troubled relationship? When you use the elements in this book as building blocks to create a strong and stable tower of love, both spouses feel cared for and appreciated. Both spouses understand and invest in the marriage wisely. Both are aware of principles that reveal and rebuild continually from any weaknesses and vulnerabilities.

Each player in the block game seeks to avoid being the one that causes the failure of the tower. We agree. We believe in adding and replacing missing elements to shore up your tower of love. We look for signs of instability, encourage each person to actively assess it, and take steps to shore up the tower. We build. We assemble, reassemble, and reinforce the blocks to make our strong and stable tower serve us as individuals and as a couple. And we are here to help you do the same thing. Recognizing instability and knowing how to add the glue that holds the pieces together is our specialty. Your tower of love is custom-built and well worth the effort to make it stand the test of time and serve as an example to others. And we sincerely wish this for you.

> Your tower of love is custom-built and well worth the effort to make it stand the test of time and serve as an example to others.

If we asked you and your spouse to stack the A-to-Z elements according to importance, you would find two very important things. First, your stack and order of importance will differ from your mate's. It will, in fact, differ from the stacks your neighbors, parents, friends, and other readers of this book would create. It will look different based on your past experiences, hopes and fears, beliefs, assumptions, seasons of life, and so much more. Secondly, your stacked elements will sometimes reprioritize and even restack themselves without notifying you or getting your permission. For example, after a betrayal, the elements of 'Loyalty' and 'Mending' would naturally move to the most important spots. After the birth of a child, the elements of 'Awareness' and 'Understanding' could assert themselves as primary.

67,108,863 Combinations

Consider this. There are sixty-seven million, one hundred and eight thousand, eight hundred and sixty-three unique combinations of how to arrange these 26 elements. Whew!

Just as each person in a marriage is unique, each marriage is also unique. We often like to remind people of this because it reveals the value of taking a custom approach to building and fortifying their tower of love.

Think about it. No one couple or relationship is the same—they are all very different because people are all very different. While it's human nature to want to place people into groups and categories, we, on the other hand, like to celebrate the individual rather than the category, type, or style.

Counseling theories, methodologies, and practices too often focus on pigeonholing people. While that can be helpful conceptually, it can be equally problematic when those classifications come to define one's identity, meaning, and story. Remember, if there are so many combinations of only 26 elements, how many more combinations can result from millions of couples? Let's acknowledge that we're all in unique circumstances.

We find greater success by focusing on the cause-and-effect of different relational dynamics and how they affect the individuals and thus, the relationship. We don't assign categories or pigeonhole couples. Our aim is to always help individuals and couples increase their own understanding and influence in making positive changes to their lives and relationships.

The Bottom Line

Your approach to love and marriage should be as unique as you are. And that is pretty darn unique.

Further, no relationship exists that doesn't take effort to build and stabilize. Wise couples know enough to work at building and stabilizing rather than waiting and working on reassembly and repair. They work to build love rather than seeking to find it.

A LOOK IN THE MIRROR

1. Where, how, and what did you learn about love and relationships in your younger years?

2. Recall a time when you had a sudden reassembling of your life values or priorities due to an event or discovery?

3. How stable or unstable would you currently consider your tower of love?

4. What are three things that make your relationship unique?

5. What are three positive things that you bring to your relationship?

6. What are three positive things that your mate brings to your relationship?

7. Who do you know that has successfully reassembled an unstable tower of love?

NOVELTY   FLEXIBILITY

HOPE

SAFETY   KNOWLEDGE

TRUST

ITY QUIETING DESIR

BELIEFS

AWARENESS   INTIMACY

PROTECT ENGAGEMENT

GRATITUDE

WORDS

TO

LOVE BY

AWARENESS

—

A well-informed interest; the ability to know and perceive, to feel, or to be cognizant of something or someone.

ARE YOU FAMILIAR WITH THE OLD MR. MAGOO CARTOONS? A quirky, elderly character, Mr. Magoo found himself in all kinds of predicaments. In one episode, he tried to deposit what he thought was cash (but was actually a bag of lettuce) into what he thought was a bank (but turned out to be a horse-betting track). He also once drove his car off the road, onto the roof of a house, and right into a hot air balloon. Yet another time, he mistook an airplane for a movie theater and ended up on a departure flight.

Mr. Magoo was the epitome of obliviousness. His comical troubles resulted from his lack of awareness about his surroundings and others. Thought to be blind or nearsighted, he was completely unaware of where he was going or what he was doing.

Many of the people we have met over the years suffer from what we consider the 'Mr. Magoo Syndrome'. It's not that they are visually impaired like Mr. Magoo, but rather that they have a figurative blindness that results in a lack of awareness that gets them into some trouble—especially in their relationships.

Awareness is the Catalyst

While the A-Z elements in this book are not listed in any particular order of importance, we will tell you that awareness is by far the most important element of all. How cool is it then, that it's the first element in the book? Awareness is the launching point for successful marriages, and without awareness, the other elements wane. It's by far the greatest weakness we find in most individuals and couples. So, it's great that we're starting with this one.

Awareness is one's ability to consider a given event, emotion, or experience from another point of reference. In a marriage, it is stepping back to look at something from your mate's perspective and to understand how they might view things differently than you do.

Humans are the only creatures that can look at two pieces of information and extract a third understanding or conclusion. This is what gives us the ability to consciously solve problems. A dog may know enough to come into the house if it's cold outside, but it wouldn't know how to turn up the thermostat, put on a sweater, or build a fire (let alone light it).

What we're talking about is the connection between one's associated experiences (feelings) and the logical awareness of how they impact and color your mind, emotions, and will—both in yourself and others. This doesn't just apply with your partner; it applies with your family, friends, others, and even with yourself.

Awareness is much like a muscle. The more one uses it, the stronger it gets. Likewise, the more you practice with it, the better you get.

> Awareness is much like a muscle. The more one uses it, the stronger it gets. Likewise, the more you practice with it, the better you get.

This entire book is about being more aware of yourself, your mate, your patterns, and your marriage. Awareness isn't simply knowing more about yourself and your partner. It's about understanding the linkages and being sensitive to the need to slow things down and gain a different perspective. It's understanding your own limitations (physically, mentally, and emotionally) and working to either improve them or at least acknowledge that you have them.

Awareness Isn't Just Information

An interesting article published a few years ago reports that there is more information printed in a daily copy of a major newspaper than the average 12th Century person was exposed to in a lifetime. The Internet lets people get more information piped into their phones, iPads, or laptops than could be found in the greatest of libraries just a few years ago. The problem is that all this information has greatly reduced our ability to be patient and process things independently. The ability (and willingness) to take two pieces of information and come up with a third, all by ourselves, is beginning to erode. The information age is impacting our social awareness. Another recent study held that children today are struggling to read facial expressions in others due to a deficiency in regular eye contact with others as they turn more to electronic communication than to face-to-face conversations.

Awareness is looking at and understanding ourselves and our mates at a much deeper level so we can authentically respond rather than simply react without understanding layers of meaning. As creatures of habit, most of our reactions to life springs from an area in the brain called the limbic system, which is also known as the fast-acting brain. It is reactionary and doesn't do much thinking. The cerebral cortex, another part of the brain, is slow-acting but an energy hog. Therefore, if your brain is presented with a challenge, and there is a ready and primed response, why would you want to expend the energy to process it in the cortex? This is where awareness comes in—understanding that there are more ways to see an event than the first impression that comes to mind.

But awareness is more than knowing or perceiving. It's being able to judge emotions and events within context. It is a critical pathway to looking deeper, bypassing the autopilot of the fast-acting limbic system. Awareness is the key to relationships, and it includes the awareness that humans are not machines processing information but creatures capable of relating to other people in a myriad of ways. This is the very heart of intimacy and connection.

Awareness is a skill one develops over time to slow down assumptions and gain a better understanding. This is why past traumas can be so hard to reprocess and resolve. Once we've become locked onto a response, we hold on to it and resist letting it go.

One of the greatest hindrances couples face lies in the very nature of being individuals who always believe that they see things correctly and can therefore appraise a situation accurately. People operate on the assumption that they have enough information to conclude that they are right. Yet, they often lack the ability to see the depth of important information that would clarify the full picture. It is understandable, even normal, to crave certainty. And in the absence of knowledge, we make judgments based on past information that our fast-acting limbic system is all too happy to supply us, even though it is likely inaccurate—at least in part.

What Makes Awareness So Hard?

Why do people lock into an opinion and stick to it so stubbornly? Why is it so hard to change? Why is it that so many people don't know why their mates feel the way they do about specific topics? And why do so many people resort to giving up and saying, "I don't know," when asked why their partners feel differently than they do? The simple answer is because they are not only judging; they also fear being judged and therefore fall back on the need to be right and correct.

Remember our fast-acting brain and how it spits out answers before we have time to determine if we've gotten enough or accurate information? That might be great in an urgent or life-threatening situation, but not so much in our day-to-day lives with our mates. Sadly, all signs point to this trend of reduced awareness gaining momentum—in the wrong direction.

Happily, people can learn and relearn new information. This ability is called neuroplasticity, and it means we can learn, adapt, and reappraise information. In computer programming, computers process through "If/Else" statements. "If" one condition is true, the computer performs some programmed action. However, if something "else" is present in combination with the condition, the computer will respond differently. The more conditions are applied, the more complex the operation. Similarly, this is how we learn everything from culture to facial cues to skills with massive complexity (and why artificial intelligence will never match the nuances of human intelligence). The problem is that it takes great willingness, dedication, and a lot of flexibility to be more aware and slow down our "if" statements in order to relate to the "else"—another person's view.

This is why the concept of intimacy is so widely integrated into the various parts of this book. It's a joining of awareness, flexibility, vulnerability, authenticity, transparency, and so much more to work as necessary puzzle pieces for externalizing and seeing things apart from our prejudgments and fast-acting limbic system.

Sadly, for many, the lack of engagement, the need for certainty, and the need to be right can often create a state of rigidity. This keeps people captive and prevents them from improving their awareness muscle. We all do it, but unless we're willing to readily accept that we don't have all the information, we'll continue unaware, believing that we're "right" and our partners are "wrong". Whatever we look for, we'll find.

If you look for all the reasons you're right, that's all you'll find. But if you're willing to look at all the reasons you may not be right (or at least not entirely right), you'll be surprised at how much more awareness you'll start to have.

Myth Buster!

It is a myth that someone cannot learn to be more aware. Like anything else we master in life, it takes practice and intentional effort. It also takes desire. Ironically, becoming someone who is more aware begins (watch this) with an *awareness* that you have room to grow.

Becoming more aware requires asking questions and then (vital part here) **listening to those answers!** Listen to digest them. Listen to understand them. Listen to empathize with them. DO NOT simply listen with the intention of responding or rebutting them.

Ask yourself how your mate might see or experience situations differently than you. Why might they interpret the same circumstances differently? Are there emotional, physical, or mental reasons that your mate might not see this in the same way as you do? Why might your mate be stressed, distracted, or unhappy (maybe even "hangry") when you feel fine? A key to growing in awareness is to stay curious.

Growing in awareness isn't just about becoming more aware of your mate and others. It's learning to be self-aware. It's knowing yourself and what you think, feel, and believe—and why. This requires asking questions (just like the ones above) of yourself.

Learning to be more aware also means learning to be humbler. It means knowing—and being okay with—not being 100% "right" about things. So many couples would be so much happier and grow so much more as a couple if both mates would abandon the idea of being "right" and instead prioritize seeing things from their mates' perspective.

The Bottom Line

Successful marriages involve two mates who are aware—of themselves, their mates, and their co-created dynamic. Awareness means accepting that we do not know everything and therefore aren't necessarily always right. It's embracing the fact that there are other points of view, experiences, emotions, and thoughts impacting situations and our willingness to listen, digest, and empathize with them.

Again, this is only the launching point of a wildly successful relationship. In the following chapters, you'll see how awareness dovetails into and interacts with each of the other elements.

A LOOK IN THE MIRROR

1. Would you describe yourself as someone who is aware?

2. Do you know why your mate feels the way they do about different things such as money, sex, family roles, their career, etc.?

3. How often do you ask your mate why they believe or feel something they believe or feel?

4. If your mate asked you why you thought and felt a certain way, could you communicate these things to them? Do you even know why you think and feel the way you do?

5. Why do you think we said that awareness will play into every other element in this book?

6. What is something you can do to begin to grow in awareness—of yourself and others?

7. How can you avoid Mr. Magoo's oblivious syndrome?

BELIEFS

A trust, faith, or confidence in something or someone.

AT THE AGE OF FOUR, JOEL BELIEVED HIS PAPER AIRPLANE WOULD fly if only he could light the paper straw (the engine) that he had carefully glued to the aft of his expertly designed craft. Since this was during the height of the 60s space race, and every rocket he'd seen launched into space had a large flame propelling it, it seemed perfectly reasonable.

When he approached his dad to assist in testing this breakthrough design, he was informed that lighting the straw would only set the whole thing on fire. Nevertheless, after days of badgering by the young Joel, his dad agreed to let him test fly his creation. He was convinced his father's insistence to wet down the back yard with the garden hose was nonsense, since he was sure the paper plane would immediately be sent aloft the moment the straw was lit.

The big moment came after dinner. With trembling hands, little Joel held the paper airplane and pointed it into the sky, waiting excitedly. His dad struck the match and lit the paper straw! But instead of the plane shooting into the sky, as Joel believed it would, it went up in flames!

Despite Joel's deep belief that the plane would fly by the power of the fire, the result was that it takes much more than fire to propel flight, even in a paper airplane.

Have you ever believed in something as strongly as the five-year-old Joel believed, only to realize later that you were wrong? And that you didn't have enough information to make an informed opinion or decision?

If we are to grow and develop throughout our lives, we must understand our beliefs and accept when it's appropriate to change or adapt them. It's a significant skill and a distinguishing part of one's life journey.

Mindset Work

Mindset work is common in business circles and the self-help arena. But it is often underutilized in counseling and mentoring successful marriages. The healthiest, most resilient relationships have a positive marriage mindset and accompanying supporting beliefs—and not just a belief in marriage. The supporting beliefs encompass ideas, thoughts, notions, habits, patterns, deservedness, ability to trust, and your thoughts about yourself and others, including your mate.

Mindset work begins by looking at your beliefs. Why? Because beliefs are the frames of reference by which all your thoughts, ideas, actions, and expectations are filtered. Beliefs shape your view of the world and how you interpret and respond to thoughts and events in your life. They are the tinted lenses by which you view your world.

Exploring your beliefs can be challenging. Heck, who are we kidding? Exploring your beliefs can be downright freaking scary! If done right, you will have to deal with old wounds, hurts, insecurities, deep-seated fears, and other dark muck. Our beliefs can be buried under some serious manure and hidden in some dark, damp, scary places. Sometimes they can be found hanging out at the surface and easily recognized when a light is shone on them, but that doesn't necessarily make them easier to navigate! You will likely have to get dirty trying to uncover and evaluate them. But it is worth it. The strongest couples are made up of two people that have beliefs working for their marriage, not against.

Uncovering Those Beliefs

We have an enlightening exercise that we complete with most of our clients to help reveal the various beliefs that are working for and against a wildly successful marriage. Below is a version of that exercise so you can do it too. We customize the questions for each client to help zero in on and uncover beliefs that seem to be hindering them, and we do this live (in person or by phone). We start sentences for them and ask them to complete the sentences out loud and quickly. When completing the sentences, it's important to go with your first thought or response and not to think about what the "right answer" is. There is no judgment about being right or wrong, but it is very important that your responses be authentic. The goal is to uncover your beliefs so you can understand the underlying role they play in your life.

EXERCISE

Complete the following sentences that have been started.

Life is_____.

Money is_____.

Marriage is_____.

Forgiveness is_____.

Husbands should always_____.

Husbands should never_____.

Wives should always_____.

Wives should never_____.

Divorce is_____.

Conflict in a healthy relationship is_____.

Every marriage needs_____.

Marriages succeed because_____.

Marriages fail because_____.

Marriages last because_____.

Children come before_____.

STOP: Did you complete the exercise on beliefs above? Please do not skip this step or rush through it.

After you complete the exercise, review your answers. Put a plus next to the ones that you think are positive and supportive of a wildly successful marriage. Put a minus by the ones that undermine a marriage. And for any that you think are neutral, leave blank or put a 0 next to it.

Would you say that your responses are more supportive or unsupportive of a successful marriage? Are some of your beliefs in conflict with each other?

Remember that your belief(s) about something will dictate, to a large degree, your level of success in that area. They will cause you to experience each conversation, action, idea, and interaction through the filter of that belief. Sometimes this is good and sometimes not so much.

For example, if someone believes they have no chance of success at a task, they will probably never try or sabotage themselves by giving up too soon. We all know very capable people that underachieve or sabotage when they could be more successful.

The good news is that beliefs can be changed. Think about a time in your life that you realized you were wrong and had to change your opinion. Or a time that you got additional information and it changed your perspective, just like the four-year-old Joel with his paper plane.

Perhaps you can relate to the following story from some of our former clients. Of course, some details such as names have been changed, but you might resonate with their perspectives.

Lena and Rob

Lena grew up in a broken home. Her father had abandoned her, her mother, and her two siblings when she was about 12. Times were tough after he left, and she often took care of her younger siblings while her mother worked. They frequently did without. She remembers her mother often saying, "You can't trust men to take care of their family."

Lena and Rob had been happily married for five years—happily until the last six months before things began to unravel. They found themselves arguing about nearly everything, according to Rob. Rob claimed that Lena became more distant and "snappy" when they started talking about having kids. He knew her past and thought he was sensitive to it. He thought he was aware. He constantly tried to reassure her that he was not her dad. But the more they talked about having kids, the worse things got.

They found themselves arguing about things like never before: money, work, retirement, vacation spots, friends, family—even buying a new car became a war. You name it, and they were arguing about it.

After a few sessions and some belief work, it was discovered that Lena had the deeply rooted and guiding belief that men really can't be trusted to take care of their families. Sure, they were both aware that she had learned to be less trusting in her past, but she didn't even realize how deep the roots of this belief went and that it became a guiding principle in her life. In part, they didn't realize it because they hadn't gotten serious about starting a family until then. But when the conversations got real, the belief made its way to the forefront and began showing itself through Lena's resistance to Rob.

Lena wanted to start a family with Rob and wanted to be a mother. But her belief that men can't be trusted trumped her desire to start a family with Rob. She sincerely believed that *she* needed to get to a career level where she could financially take care of herself and a child just in case Rob didn't do his part as a father. So, naturally, talking about having kids before she felt she was at the point where she could support herself and a child without him was going to cause conflict. This guiding principle was an unconscious, internal vow. We make them all the time, often unknowingly, just as Lena did.

Interestingly, Lena would tell you herself that Rob was the most loyal and loving man she had ever known. She didn't believe he would ever leave her, and instead believed that they could work out any problem. When two beliefs crash head on, which one wins? The one that you didn't know was there. Beliefs are sneaky like that.

Unknown Beliefs

Our unknown beliefs can be like suckers that grow at the base of a tree. At first, they may look like the rest of the tree, but eventually it becomes apparent that they aren't. Suckers grow from trees that may appear strong and healthy but suffer some unseen stress. The sucker grows as a tree attempts to develop new branches/tree for survival, but it ultimately puts more stress on the tree and depletes it of its energy and resources. Unknown beliefs can do the same. They may have developed from some past experiences as an attempt to survive or adapt, but left to their own, they can drain us. We may appear healthy for a while, but these undiscovered beliefs that we haven't dealt with will eventually take a toll on us.

Thankfully, Rob and Lena are on track now and reportedly trying to get pregnant. They're working to overcome her beliefs together. Therapy was needed to work through the associations and beliefs.

Sometimes just the realization of the belief is enough to bring it to light, so it isn't lurking in the shadows and causing so much fear. In Rob and Lena's case, having the belief in the open meant that if some trigger came up, they could talk about it. It was not seen as a weakness or a fault. And after a couple of months, they started to laugh about the occasional twinges.

Changing Our Beliefs

Beliefs can be learned, unlearned, and relearned. Beliefs can be downgraded or updated. This is the power of growth and why it is so important to challenge your beliefs.

It is valuable to understand how insidious our beliefs can be and to understand that our beliefs are about the story of the story (the internal narratives we tell ourselves).

The limbic system, as discussed, is the heart of our emotional system. We talk about it in **R is for Regulation**, too. Sometimes people will call it the "lizard" or "reptile" brain because it's considered to be paleomammalian—meaning it is part of an old, quick-reacting system looking for anything that might do us harm.

Our limbic system also helps us do things out of habit and association, which can be good or bad. Think about that time you drove to work and didn't recall the journey because you were busy thinking of other things. Or the time that you started to drive to work, out of habit, but had intended to go somewhere else. You have the limbic system to thank for those times—it likes habits. It's kind of like your smartphone—when you leave the house in the morning, it predicts where you're headed and gives you the best routes and arrival time based on your past patterns.

Further, the limbic system is the holding space for your beliefs and habits. It doesn't discern between fact, fallacy, past, present, or future. It is a fast-acting part of your brain and jumps to conclusions, often with little information, or pulls from information stored long ago that may or may not apply to the current situation. Understandably, the limbic system also manages our fight, flight, or freeze responses.

Modern day offices have abandoned the Rolodex, but offices before the 1980s relied heavily on these small, 2" x 3" removable paper inserts set upon a rolling wheel—they provided quick access to information and were easy to change or expand. Before the days of search engines, where you can now access whatever information your heart desires, it was much harder to find, store, and access information. Therefore, one would put contact, business, vendor, and additional information on the Rolodex cards for easy future reference.

Rolodexes were sorted alphabetically, but our brain's internal Rolodex is grouped by topics like betrayal, abandonment, affection, and loss, which can be triggered by a smell, a song, a color, or other things. Just like the removable inserts in the Rolodex, we can update our limbic system "cards" (beliefs). We can remove, add, or write over the beliefs we created from our experiences. Of course, it takes effort and awareness (there's that word again). Even a little boy who gets burned on a stove and becomes afraid can later become a professional chef if he can successfully overwrite his negative childhood association with stoves and cooking.

Here's another helpful visual. For each belief you have, imagine that you have a scale, something like the scales of justice, in which one side can be weighted down more than the other (or the two sides can be even). For each belief, whichever side of the scale is tipped will compel you to act out that belief or find information to support it. If one side is heavily weighted, you may even be compelled to ignore contradictory information to support your belief. The more intense a situation, the more weight or "umph" is applied to prove to yourself that you're right.

It is natural to associate current events with past experiences. We are constantly evaluating, judging, and using our collection of experiences to judge, grade, evaluate, and determine if the outcome of the current event has already been decided. Interestingly, research suggests that much of what we believe comes by proxy. More of our beliefs may have been caught than taught. We learn by watching others and by seeing events that cause us to make judgments.

Of course, it is normal to want certainty and a simplified world. But there is value in delving into beliefs and discovering if they need modification. There is also value in marital conflict, which helps you reevaluate your beliefs and, more importantly, work through them. This is why we selected **Conflict** for element **C**!

Do these beliefs hit home for you?

Here are some beliefs that come up often in our practices. Consider if they are ones that you hold, too. And are they leading you toward or away from a wildly successful marriage?

- Do you believe that marriages have an expiration date?
- Do you subscribe to the "Starter Marriage" philosophy?
- Do you believe that if your mate would just change, everything would be ok? Or that no change is required on your part?
- Are you more focused on being right than happy?
- Do you believe that your way is the only right way?
- Do you believe that you can't recover from a betrayal in your marriage?
- Do you believe that sex is dirty or only for procreation?
- Do you believe that kids come first, even before your mate?

What if you find that your beliefs, values, and scales need adjustment? Well, it means that you're just human like all the other nearly 8 billion people on Earth. The values that we hold at the ages of 10, 20, 30, 40, etc., will evolve, as will our accompanying beliefs.

Remember the story of the little boy who became afraid of cooking? After his negative experience with a stove as a child, he evaluated and believed that stoves were unsafe. But as an adult with more knowledge, awareness, and maturity, he learned to respect a hot stove but also see it as a tool. You can't caramelize an onion without heat, and he learned and accepted more information about cooking until he replaced his belief that stoves would only hurt him. He became a world class chef and his efforts led him to a fuller, richer life.

Because our beliefs morph with new information, time, knowledge, experiences, and awareness, we should put effort into understanding how they affect all our relationships and how we can change them when desired. As the boy grew into a man, that's what he had to do to achieve his dreams as a chef.

The Bottom Line

Our beliefs impact the way we view our lives and other people. We operate and make daily decisions and judgments based on those beliefs—even when many of them are deep-rooted and quite possibly unknown to us. It's important to dive deep into our beliefs about a variety of things: ourselves, others, marriage, and relationships. While it isn't easy—or always pretty—to confront our deep-seated beliefs, it is crucial to the health and vitality of our marriages.

> When we identify what drives our motivations, judgments, and responses, we can control whether to keep them, change them, or toss them.

Just as our outlook on many aspects of life can change from childhood through adulthood and into retirement age, our deep beliefs can also change. When we identify what drives our motivations, judgments, and responses, we can control whether to keep them, change them, or toss them.

A LOOK IN THE MIRROR

1. Did you complete the beliefs activity/questionnaire in this chapter? What did you learn about yourself from it?

2. Did your mate complete it? Was anything surprising to you about their responses?

3. In what area(s) do you and your mate differ in your beliefs?

4. Identify a time in your life when you changed your mind about something you believed. What prompted the change? How have you grown from this change?

5. Were there any elements of Lena's and Rob's story that you could identify with?

6. When has someone else's situation or experience molded your own beliefs?

7. Are there any Rolodex cards (beliefs) that you need to purge to create a fuller life?

CONFLICT

—

The tension that is created between two opposing needs, wants, or desires within a relationship.

SHAKESPEARE, SPIELBERG, HOWARD, AND MORE—THEY ALL KNEW one thing. A play, film, novel, etc., cannot sell out theaters or top charts unless it contains one very crucial piece. The works cannot captivate our attention, warm our hearts, and live on for generations if that one important aspect is missing. And that is conflict. No great story is ever told without some sort of conflict. The hero isn't the hero without a conflict. The happy ending is not a happy ending without at least working through one conflict to give the main characters some obstacles to overcome.

> We say that conflict creates depth and opens the doors to the greatest stories ever told—even your own marriage's love story.

Yet, so many people view conflict as something to avoid or something disastrous to end all good. Well, we disagree. We say that conflict creates depth and opens the doors to the greatest stories ever told—even your own marriage's love story.

If you turn on the television, peruse social media, or even drive your car down the busiest streets, you'll become painfully aware that conflict is all around. In every good story, the ones that inspire us, some great conflict is always woven into the fabric of the narrative. Life is really about conflict and our ability to overcome it. So, why be surprised that our marriages also have their fair share of conflict? In fact, no other relationship has potential for more conflict than a marriage! You live together, sleep together, have kids, share meals and chores, and go on vacations together. The number of things that can get cross-threaded with our partners is infinite. We have often heard couples say, "I don't seem to have these kinds of problems with people at work, but when I come home, I do with YOU!" Meaning, "Everybody at work loves me, so it must be you, not me!" Of course, we then ask, "How many of your coworkers do you share a bed, finances, or household chores with?" Marriage is a whole different animal. Conflict is unavoidable in a healthy relationship.

The letters and associated words in the chapters of this book are meant to be the positive aspects of a healthy relationship, or at least they are meant to be values we believe are favorable to a strong and thriving relationship. However, if you ask most couples how they feel about conflict, they will generally say that it's something they'd like to avoid at all costs. Most will go far and wide to keep from being entangled in conflict. We, however, would like to make a case that conflict is inherently not a good or bad thing, but really the only method to grow a healthy relationship. Conflict can either be used to build up a relationship or destroy it.

When we talk about conflict, we're talking about the healthy kind— the kind that causes you to face difficult issues and resolve them; the kind that makes you grow stronger like exercise does. Most counseling methods work to reduce conflict, but we work to increase it! Seems counterintuitive, doesn't it? But, in the absence of conflict, relationships will stagnate and grow cold. The important thing to remember about conflict is that we all have it, and it can be very helpful in taking you to places you'd never take yourself. It can build your relationship up or tear it down. Simply put, it can't be avoided, yet most couples go out of their way to do just that.

The Dimensions of Conflict

Conflict is measured in two dimensions: intensity and duration. Intensity is the level of how emotionally engaged one gets in the conflict. Use a scale from zero to ten. Anything over a five is considered fighting. We work to help couples stay under a five by empowering them to develop effective strategies. Duration is the other crucial component, typically measured in minutes, hours, or days. We've also seen it measured in years, and yes, sadly, even in decades. Productive conflict should be kept under five in intensity and should be resolved within hours or at least within a few days. Anything outside of that starts to damage the level of confidence one or both will have toward the trust and safety of the relationship

Most therapists address conflict by trying to get clients to negotiate a compromise in which neither person gets everything they want, but both can hopefully live with what they get. While that sounds good in business, when it comes to intimate relationships, we see this as two people losing. We advocate for win-win solutions where the outcome of conflict produces a better outcome than what either person wanted from the onset of the conflict. When couples find those outcomes, conflict is no longer feared or avoided, but embraced.

Embracing conflict is a skill that needs to be developed rather than a concept to memorize. Every couple is uniquely different, and each relationship co-creates a pattern of managing conflict that is unique to them. This is why many therapeutic approaches, in our opinion, fall short of delivering to couples the skills they need. Couples don't only need to co-create a healthy understanding; they also need the willingness to embrace the co-creative process so that they become comfortable with being uncomfortable in the dance of conflict. People can go to a marriage retreat, read a book, or even go to counseling. All of these can be good, but they are all events. What we advocate for is a process that needs to be learned and developed by the couple.

Like many other elements in this book, before you can deal with conflict effectively, you have to have an understanding of authenticity, transparency, and vulnerability. These, along with other concepts like flexibility and awareness, are the cornerstones needed for a couple to learn the art and dance of effective, healthy conflict. People often come to counseling to work on conflict resolution, but too often have no desire to relate to or understand themselves, let alone their partner. They just want their partner to do things their way.

We've come to believe that one of the universal human conditions is that we all think we're right! People believe their understanding is spot on and that they have taken all the needed information into account. They have left nothing out. Not only that, they believe their perception of what the other person thinks or feels is also spot on! Yes, we all seem to believe that we have absolute clarity of the facts. The only problem is that when you get people to authentically relate to each other, they discover that life and their partner are far more complex than their generalizations or beliefs. Human relationships are too complex and messy to effectively process conflict with a simple, singular view of what the truth is.

So, why do people get so stuck in conflict? This is a topic that is more important to understand than how to manage conflict itself. In fact, most people do a great job of managing conflict. The problem is that they often don't resolve anything. And what they create is not greater understanding and closeness, but rather more hurt feelings, bitterness, and resentment. Our initial goal when we work with couples is to first help them understand how their conflict impacts their ability to resolve their issues.

Most people are familiar with the book *Love Languages* by Gary Chapman. In it, he outlines what he sees as the five ways people give and wish to receive love. It's a great resource in understanding yourself and your partner. Simply put, people love in the "language" they want to be loved in. It's a simple but effective concept. The five love languages are Time, Touch, Words of Affirmation, Gifts, and Acts of Service. So, if you happen to feel best loved from receiving tender words, but your partner feels best loved from receiving a tender touch, you both will tend to misunderstand the needs of the other. What does this have to do with conflict? Well, what if you were to learn that there is also a language of conflict that's just as alive and well within your relationship? To demonstrate this, we've developed an analogy called the Conflict Box!

The Conflict Box

Imagine a box with four corners, each one representing a place that you retreat to when it's time to manage a conflict. The problem with these corners is that we see them as ways to leverage control or power in conflict. In reality, they are the very things that prevent us from resolving it. Instead of conflict being used to build up and fortify your relationship, it ends up tearing it down. When people get into one of these corners, they will tend to press hard into their corner, and if that doesn't work, they will often jump to another corner. When couples do this, they are in a cycle of unhealthy conflict that often gets too intense and drags on for far too long—sometimes for years!

So, let's examine these four corners. The first thing to understand is that each corner is on a continuum or scale. You might be in one of these corners a little or a lot, so *your mileage may vary* from others who share the same corner as you. And, we all have a corner we tend to favor. You'll need to actively work to keep yourself out of yours if you ever want to have a wildly successful marriage.

Villain Corner: The villain, bully, or prosecutor is the person who always points the finger of judgment. The villain is the one that is generally first to blame, accuse, or criticize, often with little, if any, ability to see themselves or their contribution to the issue. They believe they are the standard by which things within the relationship should be measured. They are often very rigid and stuck in their belief that they are correct, and the problem is the fault of others. It's hard to resolve conflict from this corner since the person in it lacks the willingness to be empathetic or relate to the other person, including that they may see, feel, and interpret things very differently.

Avoider Corner: The avoider is best described as the person who attempts to avoid conflict by blending into the wall, shutting down emotionally, or retreating. It's difficult to resolve conflict with someone who isn't there. This person will often choose to avoid conflict to try to minimize event(s). They often fear confrontation and can disengage to the point of shutting down emotionally or stonewalling. They have a fear of engaging and struggle to express themselves authentically. The more their partner engages, the more the avoider retreats. Avoiders resist being fully known, often due to a lack of feeling secure in and with others close to them. Yet the avoider's unwillingness to participate leaves their partner feeling unloved, unvalued, abandoned, or disrespected.

Victim Corner: The victim is the person who is easily offended and hurt by their partner and others. They will tend to weaponize their hurt/pain to gain a moral high ground in the relationship. They often don't take any responsibility—after all, they've been hurt, and it's the fault of the person who hurt them! They've not accepted that their feelings are their own responsibility; and rather than take back their power, they find power in taking on the role of victim. Sadly, this is a common pattern when couples get stuck in conflict. Much like the villain, the victim rarely takes responsibility for how they feel. People that cling to the victim corner have typically done this much of their lives. This keeps them firmly stuck. We've also seen this in people who refuse to forgive, reminding their partner frequently of all the things they're doing wrong, and feeling justified in withholding trust.

Pleaser Corner: The pleaser corner is the last corner, and most of us would find nothing wrong with wanting to please a partner. The problem with the pleaser is that they are not doing it out of a sense of caring, but out of a need to be validated. They are the quintessential codependent in the relationship. They're okay if you're okay, so they spend much of their time working to be validated. In their noble efforts to be seen and appreciated, they lack the ability to hold others accountable and will work tirelessly to make others happy until they become exhausted and move to another corner. This tendency was the inspiration for the *Boundaries* book series by Dr. Henry Cloud and Dr. John Townsend.

By the way, while the Pleasers may need more and clearer boundaries, we don't ardently support more boundaries for the first three corners—they don't need more boundaries, they are already entrenched in their corners!

Regardless of what your conflict is, if you can't resolve it or draw closer to one another through a process, chances are that you're in one or more of these corners and need to move towards the center.

It's most important to be able to identify the corner you favor and see the way in which it keeps you from effectively resolving your conflict. Most conflicts are likely just do-overs of previous conflicts. The names and details of yours may change, but the emotions and feelings are all still pretty much the same, much like a recurring dream that eventually becomes a nightmare. The only way out of the conflict box is through awareness and willingness: awareness of your own corners combined with the willingness to step out of the box. If not, you and your partner will keep reinforcing those old automatic responses, even though they only delivered momentary successes while serving to reinforce feelings of being misunderstood, disrespected, and unloved, leaving you hopelessly stuck.

Thinking about the conflict corners, can you see how they play a part in your relational conflicts, those of your parents, and others?

The process we use to move couples past their conflict patterns is more complicated than we can cover in this chapter. It's complicated because we must customize it to the individuals we are working with. It's not a one-size-fits-all approach. As we indicate throughout this book, we all need to address different issues and patterns based on our personalities and past experiences in life. Wildly successful marriages are not made by following a checklist or simply going to a weekend marriage retreat (although we offer those and think there can be great value in them). No, they are built by learning how to embrace the fear and hesitance that keeps so many from ever fully seeing and being seen by their partners. Instead, many of us choose to attack, stonewall, blame, and fail to set healthy limits in our relationship(s). The truth is that you don't have to stick with what you've always done. You can do something different. Finding your personal power to positively affect your relationship is one of the most rewarding things you can do. And conflict is the vehicle that can take you there if you learn to better understand how to do it.

Another thing to consider is the level of conflict a couple engages in. People may judge how much a high-conflict couple fights, but we contend that high-conflict couples are often better than no-conflict couples when it comes to the potential for creating a wildly successful marriage. When couples come to counseling and are still willing to fight, they are still engaged. When they've gotten to the point over time where they stop fighting completely, they simply don't care anymore. The opposite of love is apathy, you see. Couples in apathy are difficult to get to reengage, and often those relationships are the hardest to save.

The Bottom Line

Conflict exists in every walk of life, and in fact is quite necessary. It's neither good or bad, but necessary in creating depth as you write and live your own love story, and the very fact that you're in an intimate relationship creates a myriad of opportunities for conflict.

Instead of going on the defensive or claiming that you're "right" and your mate's "wrong," develop the skills of communicating better and finding win/win outcomes that give both of you an even better resolution than you'd wanted in the first place. Maybe you think your mate is asking for apples when you gave them oranges, but they're really asking for eggs! There are a million ways to communicate, so get comfortable with taking the necessary time to see what your mate is saying, feeling, or thinking. And learn to express your own needs, desires, and perspectives in a way that invites more conversation and understanding. Remember the Love Languages—some people don't even use words to express their feelings.

Conflict isn't the end of the world and doesn't have to erode your relationship over time. If you're open and flexible, it will deepen your trust in each other and make your marriage even stronger.

A LOOK IN THE MIRROR

1. What corner of the conflict box do you favor? Why?
2. What corner of the conflict box does your mate favor? Why?
3. How does your and your mate's conflict style interact?
4. Where did you learn how to navigate conflict in your relationship?
5. How would you rate the current level of conflict in your relationship?
6. What is one thing you can do to move toward the center of the conflict box?
7. What is the value of learning how to stay neutral and in the center of the conflict box?

DESIRE

—

The emotion of longing or hoping for a person, object, or outcome.

A COLLEAGUE INTRODUCED US TO THE YOUTUBE SENSATION THAT IS Eric Thomas, aka ET the Hip Hop Preacher. One of his trending videos is from a speech he made to students at Michigan State University. His motivational speech was primarily about success, but he kept coming back to the same question, "How bad do you want it?" We think he was getting at exactly how much desire they had to succeed.

American self-help author Napoleon Hill says it so wonderfully: *"Desire is the starting point of all achievement, not a hope, not a wish, but a keen pulsating desire which transcends everything."* Whatever it is that you want to achieve or succeed at, desire must be your starting point. And yes, as you can imagine, desire has much to do with whether we succeed in our relationships, too.

Your Desire Level

One of the first things that we assess when a couple comes in for counseling is their level of desire to improve or save their marriage. Gauging where each person is on the desire continuum is important. The level of desire can range from a strong desire to create and keep a healthy marriage to not caring at all (complete apathy) and being ready to toss it.

When a couple gets married, each partner brings in their own array of hopes, dreams, thoughts, and ideas: ideas about what marriage is and isn't, what it will or won't look like in the future, and what effort it will or won't take to sustain. It is rare for two people to marry and immediately long to get divorced or separated. Instead, we find that most who marry are hopeful and desirous of a successful marriage: one in which the mutual needs of both people are met, and they each feel supported, loved, appreciated, and encouraged to grow and become all they can be, both as individuals and as partners.

The desire for a successful marriage plays out distinctly differently for each couple, just as one couple's definition of success will vary from another couple's. One person will seek wisdom through podcasts or advice from books like this one. And another might seek wisdom via prayer. Some couples reach out and seek help at the first sign of trouble. Some wait until their marriage is in hospice to consider outside help. Some let their marriage coast until they're in rough waters, while a neighboring couple is always looking for opportunities to strengthen their marriage and support their mate. What success looks like to one couple will look different to others. As such, one couple's approach to co-creating a successful marriage will be distinguishably different from the approach of other couples.

Grab the Thermometer

We, however, are less concerned with the specifics of how you approach creating your wildly successful marriage. In **E is for Engagement**, we talk more about using the act of engaging as a way to assess and improve your marriage. It's more important to consistently gauge where you are and know what causes the dial to move up or down. Think of it like a thermometer. You don't want it to read too low or frostbite sets in. And, if it's too high, you risk overheating. Much like a fever is a sign that our bodies are in a battle with illness, being too high on the desire scale can indicate signs of dis-ease. But, again, much like a body fighting an illness will raise its temperature, couples battling for a struggling marriage might see their desire for the marriage go up.

A basic desire for a successful marriage is crucial. Your feelings, effort, engagement, and willingness to forge ahead are all filtered through the level of desire that you have to create a wildly successful marriage and your beliefs about that. A strong desire fuels one's efforts to move forward. It tints the lens in which you see challenges, disagreements, and conflict. It dictates whether you look for the worst or the best in a situation and even how much grace and forgiveness you offer your partner.

A strong desire for a successful marriage leads one to see their mate's noble intentions. You recognize that you not only want what is best for your mate, but likewise, your mate wants what is best for you. Conversely, a low desire for the marriage, whether coming from you or your partner, can lead one to dismiss noble intentions and only focus on the negative. It discourages couples from working through the rough patches and causes people to see only the battles and disappointments. It creates the tone, "Why bother?"

Whether you are at one extreme or the other in your desire for creating a thriving marriage, it's valuable to look at why. If you feel overly desirous, it can cause you to become unsafe, a doormat, or unrealistic without healthy boundaries with your mate. A low desire for a thriving marriage is likely because you feel hopeless after past efforts. Perhaps your partner has been unfaithful in some way, and your lack of desire for your marriage is a protective measure; or you are disillusioned and just don't see them in the same light anymore. Pssst: Even after severe betrayal, not all hope has to be lost. If a couple is willing to do the work, they can be stronger and happier even after a significant betrayal. Trust us, we've seen it done repeatedly.

Yea, Nay, or Delay

Let us let you in on a secret. It only takes *one* person to work to save a marriage and make course corrections to impact the marriage and their partner. Yes, the ultimate success of marriage requires both of you, but just one of you can start steering your marriage in a positive direction and that may make all the difference. Your goal should not be to change your partner, but your partner will likely respond to your actions, words, and behavior, which gives you the ability to influence change in your partner.

We teach struggling couples the idea of yea, nay, or delay. At any point in time, each partner's desire for the marriage can be in one of three states: yea, nay, or delay. This means you are either all in and committed to making your marriage succeed (yea), you've decided you're out (nay), or you've opted to not decide just yet and delay. Sadly, if your mate is nay, you are facing an uphill battle. You can't be all in if they aren't. While you may still desire and work for your marriage's success, you cannot be in a marriage if the other person ends it. But you can be in delay— waiting to see what they decide, waiting to make a major decision, waiting to see what it is you should choose. And delay is okay, but it's not a long-term solution. In the short-term, delay can be a better option than nay.

If you're leaning towards the nay or delay side, it's important to consider the value of shared history in your decision. Shared history includes the inside jokes, funny memories, memorable moments from the past, traditions, and even the things that, at the time, went awry but now inspire looking back with fondness, smiles, or humor. It's like a comedian circling back to an earlier joke and giving the audience a chance to relive it. It's an often overlooked but critical area to review before deciding on divorce. Clients usually undervalue the loss of shared history and often report that they didn't realize how long it would take to rebuild it with a new partner.

Shared history strengthens relationships if we let it. It builds confidence and capacity. Shared history can also allow us to see how bad things were and yet got repaired. Today's troubles can turn into tomorrow's shared history. Shared history can serve to turn the desire dial for marriage up higher and allow the meaning of an event to change over time. Much like an ending of a movie can change the meaning of the beginning scene. Shared history also builds our limbic system and reminds us that we can get through this and solve our issues. This is why focusing on fond memories—rather than focusing on the bad ones—is necessary to keep the desire for marriage high. We're not saying you should ignore the bad past experiences or become like an ostrich with its head in the sand; rather, perhaps a bit of delaying and reframing is just the key that's needed.

Being Goal-Oriented

In solution-focused theory, the approach to counseling is goal-oriented. The attention is focused not on the problem(s), but rather on finding solutions and achieving goals. When properly deployed, the "miracle question" is a powerful, solution-focused technique. It goes something like this:

> *"Suppose that you were to wake up tomorrow morning and a miracle had happened. Yet, you didn't know that it had happened. The miracle is that the issues you were having in your marriage were corrected, and everything was now great in your marriage. What's the first thing you would notice if the miracle had happened? What would be different? How long would it take to notice and what would have happened or not happened to let you know this miracle took place? How would you feel or behave differently? And how would you interact differently with your partner?"*

The answer to these questions can bring about fresh insight as to what is needed to change and jumpstart the process. It can help foster a desire to create a wildly successful marriage. It allows one to be hopeful, and that hope is spurred by the desire for a miracle marriage—because you believe it can happen!

Sources of Desire

The source of your desire for a successful marriage can come from a lot of different places. Your motivation and desire may exist because your parents modeled a great marriage. Maybe you grew up watching them, and you want the same thing. You know it's possible because you've seen it. You know the life it provided for you and your siblings, and you want to give the same thing to your kids. If this is you, thank your parents for their example.

On the flip side, maybe your parents had a troubled marriage and it ended in a nasty, bitter divorce. Maybe this has made you determined to redeem marriage and have a dream marriage and be role models for your children. Perhaps you remember what it was like as a kid, and you want to help your kids avoid that pain and confusion.

Maybe your desire for a successful marriage stems from somewhere else: your love and longing for you mate, your religious beliefs, your goals for the future, or maybe even something you read in a book like this one. Whatever the fuel for your desire-fire, keep it burning, and take the actions necessary to make it happen. Keep adding to the fire and adding fuel before you are down to ash and embers. It is much easier to keep a fire burning than it is to start a fire or revive one that's nearly out.

> Whatever the fuel for your desire-fire, keep it burning, and take the actions necessary to make it happen.

Lost Desire, Apathy, and Heartache

If your desire for creating and sustaining a strong marriage has waned, consider the reasons. Eroded trust, boredom, and disillusionment can all play a part. Also, consider how long your desire has been waning. When Kimberly does discernment counseling with her clients, she always asks her clients about when and why the desire started to wane. This helps to know the needed steps to proceed.

Some couples have moved beyond a loss of desire and are indeed in heartache. In these cases, it is understandable to want to end the pain. Use caution, however, when considering easing the heartache via divorce. Sadly, statistics report that divorce regret (or at least "not trying harder" regret) can be as high as 50%. Understand that your value system today may not be tomorrow's. We have worked with so many couples who say they wish they had stayed in and fought for their marriage. You likely won't regret fighting to keep the marriage desire alive, but you could regret not fighting for it. Repairing a marriage, although it may take a lot of work, can also help make the heartache stop; and sometimes, divorce just swaps out the problems and heartache. Of course, if you're not safe, your safety is always a priority, and not all marriages can be or should be saved.

The Bottom Line

Every action, word, thought, and prayer you put into making your marriage successful stems from a desire to do so. You have to want it. You have to really, really, really want it and not stop wanting it. Seasons in marriage and levels of desire may ebb and flow, but we have to be willing to gauge where we are and where our mate is so we can steer our relationship back in the right direction.

A LOOK IN THE MIRROR

1. Where are you on the desire thermometer? Are you hot, cold, or somewhere in between?

2. Where is your mate? Is their desire for a thriving marriage evident to you?

3. How do you recognize when your desire for your marriage is waning? What are the tells?

4. Consider the miracle question: What would it look like to wake up tomorrow to your dream marriage?

5. Ask your mate the miracle question and listen to their answer without judgment or defense.

6. If you're feeling nay or delay, why is that? And what would it take to get you back to yea?

7. What motivates your desire for your marriage to succeed?

ENGAGEMENT

Taking action to maintain or improve one's relationship with another.

IF YOU'VE EVER BEEN AROUND SMALL CHILDREN (NIECES, NEPHEWS, neighbors, or your own), you know that most kids really truly just want your time and attention. It doesn't matter what activity they're doing; they just want you to be present. They beg for someone's undivided attention. If you were at the park and on your phone, they'd call out for you to watch them swing or watch them climb. If you're around a kid watching television, they're probably sitting right up on you—hindering you from trying to read your newspaper, skim social media, or talk to another person. And should you try to fake paying attention, they know. It's like a sixth sense for kids. And they'd call you out in 2.5 seconds for it, too.

> Engagement is the outward expression of the effort one actively takes to cherish and protect the mutual relational investment.

More than anything, kids want you to be present and engaged with them in whatever activity they do. Don't believe us? Ask any preschool or elementary teacher. Kids want you to be actively in the moment with them—making memories and being fully aware of them.

Engagement in a marriage is a little bit different, but it still takes the right mindset and intentional actions. Engagement is the outward expression of the effort one actively takes to cherish and protect the mutual relational investment. It's the awareness, desire, and action that maintains a wildly successful relationship.

Myth Buster!

Engagement is one of the most often misunderstood, if not down-right dismissed, elements of a wildly successful marriage. It's more than just the desire to engage, which is also important, but engagement is regular, sustained, and active participation in one's relationship.

Many people live with the false belief that if they had only married the "right" person, everything would be great, and the relationship would run on love and no real sustained effort would need to be undertaken. Deep down, if honest, they don't believe that entirely, but many people tend to feel (and too often act) as if love and connection should just happen serendipitously.

We can assure you that's not the case. Good, meaningful relationships don't just happen. They are created and maintained, often even rebuilt or remodeled. As you've probably already heard. Most people will be in multiple marriages in their life. The key is to have them with the same person.

It Takes Elbow Grease

Engagement is the roll-up-your-sleeves elbow grease that's needed to endure tough times and achieve the marriage you both want. It's the stick-to-it-iveness to carry you through those dark valley periods and get you to the other side. Relationships have many seasons, and each one you face requires new skills to be learned and mastered. Engagement is the glue—the secret sauce— that you must have to withstand the long journey. Show us a happy marriage, and we'll show you a couple that is engaged with one another.

Case in point: A study a while back found that couples who reported being in an unhappy marriage, but stayed together, were actually happier five years later. The report says that 80% of the couples who stuck it out reported that their marriage was happier, even good, years later. That sounds unbelievable. What the survey didn't say, but what we can tell you after working with hundreds of couples, is that the couples stayed engaged and worked through their conflict to grow their relationship. They didn't just withstand their problems and changes but thrived from them.

How long should you fight for your marriage? We will tell you: as long as it takes! Again, as we've said before, not every marriage can or should be saved. But far more could not only be saved but could actually be thriving—if only the couple had both stayed engaged and working to build the marriage they both wanted.

We are living in a throwaway society where people look at the first signs of conflict as the signal to cut and run. We want the world and relationships to be just as we demand them to be, rather than working to grow, learn, and strive together to improve them.

One of the common myths that we see in relationships is the 50/50 rule. Simply put, 50/50 relationships don't work! We agree that they sound great in theory. But it's the implementation that sends people off the rails in their relationship. The main issue is the question of which one gets to judge the efforts of themselves and the other person. We tend to give ourselves more credit for our efforts and judge more harshly the efforts and execution of others. The 50/50 model also sets us up to compare each other and minimize our partner's strengths and weaknesses.

Successful marriages can be more like 70/30 or 60/40. And the 70% or 60% person is probably you, because you're the one currently putting in the effort to read this book. Yes, the 70% needs to fall onto the person putting in the greater effort! If either you or your partner is unwilling to take on the bulk of the effort, then you're probably not engaged enough.

You Can Turn the Bolt Too Tight

This is a good time to point out the other side of engagement: being overly engaged. While being under-engaged is problematic, being overly engaged is downright unhealthy and often leads to very unbalanced relationships. Think about a bolt that is tightened too tightly into a nut with a wrench. It can strip the nut—or worse, even break it.

How can one tell if they are overly engaged? It comes down to two factors that need to be looked at separately and together. The first factor is intentions, and the second is duration.

When it comes to intentions, what are yours? Are you hoping to be noticed, loved, or appreciated by others to feel better about yourself? We call this Differentiation-of-Self, meaning that you're trying to gain your meaning and identity through other people's acceptance of you. If you love me, then I must be good enough to be loved. Therefore, I must be okay! This is often seen in the classic codependent who struggles to set healthy boundaries with others and is too often used and abused. The problem with this individual is that they tend to become tired of carrying the load and at some point, have a breakdown rather than just set healthy limits.

The second aspect is duration. How long are you running at 70% and carrying the bulk of the load? If your mate had some significant setback in life or is struggling with some issue, it's not only okay, but very healthy to come alongside and support him or her. However, if your mate resists engaging for months or years or has a destructive pattern like draining the bank account, then it's time for you to proactively engage in resolving the problems.

Simply tolerating unhealthy or deleterious behavior is not good for either mate. It's not loving; it's avoidance. When you fail to engage responsibly in a bad situation, you not only teach your mate that you'll tolerate problematic behavior, but you're teaching your kids that they need to tolerate it too.

So, you can say that if you're consistently over engaged, you're really under engaged at setting limits and as such, your relationship is going to struggle.

Obstacles to Engagement

So, what are some of the classic reasons people struggle with engagement? For many, it could be that it's never been effectively modeled for them in their own family of origin. People are often exposed to extremes of engagement. Maybe you experienced over engagement or under engagement. We rarely see people who experienced families that effectively navigated and modeled engagement. Why not change this pattern in your home for your kids?

The second big reason for a lack of engagement is waiting for their partner to initiate it. People will often say, "I'll engage once the other person does," and they get into a standoff like two Old West gunfighters waiting for the other person to make the first move. This is not the wild West! This is not a standoff. This is your marriage. And that is your spouse.

Another common issue is the "I shouldn't have to" statement that is too often the result of comparing one's relationship with a host of influencers such as friends, TV, and social media, all trying to sell you on what your life would look like if only your mate were perfect! But think— who says that you aren't the one who should start the change? Who says it gets pawned off on someone else? If you recognize the need for greater engagement, why not be the one to initiate it? What greater gift of love to both your mate and you than to take the first brave steps towards a greater marriage? What a gift to give your mate—and your children!

Now, engagement needs to be a two-way street. It requires both parties to keep their needs, wants, and desires known and balanced. Too often, we look to others outside the relationship rather than to one another to decide what engagement should even look like. This is why knowing yourself and your mate is so important. The both of you get to decide what your relationship should look like.

Over the years, we've seen countless couples who've had all sorts of lifestyles and relationships. Some work and some do not. We advocate for healthy relationships defined by a balance of power, where both partners can have those difficult conversations and work through their differences as they journey to a better understanding of each other.

Gardening in Your Marriage

Outside our office window is a garden that is well-manicured and cared for regularly by a team of workers. We know that because we see them doing it each week. When we talk to couples, we'll often point out to the garden and say, "You know we live in California, which is pretty much a desert, right? How do you think that garden stays so nice? Do you think it happens on its own, or that somebody simply chose the right combinations of plants? Or do you think it's something more?"

It's a rhetorical question, of course. But the point is well served. Somebody is engaging in the maintenance routine, varied by season. This is very much like a relationship. The staff don't over or under water the plants and lawn. They aren't there every minute fretting over it. No, they know what needs to be done and put forth a balance of efforts. Each week, people come by. Sometimes they just cut the grass. Other times, they adjust the sprinklers or trim the hedges. And a couple of times a year, I've seen them fertilize the lawn. They've even cut down dead branches and planted new flowers in the spring. Much like a marriage, it takes awareness, desire, and engagement to keep it looking so beautiful. They give a consistent amount of attention, balanced and applied consistently over time.

A relationship is much like a garden. You have to put in some sustained and consistent effort, not just at the beginning, but continually, if you want to have a garden or marriage that is thriving. You have to know yourself and your mate and what both your needs are. Much like our garden, some plants have varying needs. Some need the full sun so they can grow faster, but they may also need more water as a result. Yet, in the same beautiful garden, there are plants that prefer consistent shade and don't require as much sun. If you overwater them, they can get moldy or waterlogged. What you mate needs won't match what you need—and that's okay. You are two unique, beautiful plants that complement—not compete with—one another.

Anything of value has worth because it's not easy to get. Why should a marriage be any different? If you want a wildly successful marriage, you'll need to be willing to invest lifelong engagement into it. Nothing less will do!

The Bottom Line

Engagement in your relationship requires you to be all in for the long haul. It's part of a daily choice to take whatever actions are necessary to better your marriage. Sometimes it may seem that you don't need to initiate these actions. Do it anyway. Sometimes it may seem that you have to give more effort than your mate. Fight the urge to call it unfair, and do it anyway.

Successful marriages aren't born overnight. They are the result of your continued actions day after day, month after month, year after year. So, be the best darn landscaper out there to your garden! Mow it when it needs to be mowed. Fertilize when it needs fertilization. Do the painful act of pruning as needed. And enjoy the beauty of your efforts with your mate.

A LOOK IN THE MIRROR

1. What would engagement by you look like to your mate?

2. What would engagement by your mate look like to you?

3. Who would you say typically puts in more effort? Why do you feel that way, and what would your mate say?

4. What obstacles do you face in engagement? Do you quit easily when your efforts look unmatched or unnoticed?

5. Do you have a habit of waiting for your mate to initiate? If so, why do you feel they should first?

6. How would you describe your "gardening" efforts in your marriage?

7. What are three things you can commit to doing that would create engagement in your marriage?

FLEXIBILITY

An openness to consider or reconsider another person's view, in whole or in part, before insisting that your own view is the best course of action.

D ID YOU KNOW CHICAGO'S WORLD-FAMOUS SEARS TOWER (NOW called the Willis Tower) was designed to sway? According to engineering experts, the upper floors of the building can deflect up to three feet in any direction, when faced with the high winds that come off Lake Michigan. Why? Well, it was structured that way. Imagine a piece of uncooked spaghetti sticking straight up out of the ground. If you came by and swung at it, there's a good chance it'll snap and break. Now, imagine the same piece of spaghetti but cooked and dangling from your fingers. Give that a swat and the pasta is much less likely to break. The lesson here is simple—you've got to bend a little to keep from breaking.

The same rule applies to our relationships. We must be flexible if we want to thrive. Besides awareness, we contend that flexibility with your mate is probably one of the most important elements in a wildly successful marriage. Flexibility is a willingness to constantly survey aspects of your mate and your relationship for new information before declaring it as good or bad, right or wrong. Flexibility works in close concert with awareness because without awareness, flexibility is pointless. Awareness and flexibility are the bookends of the necessary change and growth you'll be doing in a relationship.

Feeling Stuck?

When couples are struggling in their relationship, they typically report feeling "stuck". Stuck is painful. It is uncomfortable. It is not someplace people like to be. Yet, the pain that's too great or lasts too long often becomes the agent of change that propels people to take positive steps or make necessary changes. The tallest hurdle we have when it comes to achieving flexibility is understanding our own relationship to flexibility and rigidity.

> The tallest hurdle we have when it comes to achieving flexibility is understanding our own relationship to flexibility and rigidity.

Interestingly, the same traits that we found desirable in our mates when we first met, such as consistent self-confidence or fastidious organizing, can later seem like plain old bullheadedness or rigidity. Likewise, what we once viewed as signs of a free spirit or an openness to try new things can look more like being scattered, flaky, and unreliable years later. Understanding our relationship with flexibility (and rigidity) is about coming to terms with our own views on how things should be, what should change, and how to change it. We need to understand our own approach to the process of change.

Understanding the Spectrum

Flexibility can best be thought of as a continuum with two extremes on opposite sides: overly compliant or too rigid. In high school chemistry, we are taught about the three states of water, which are gas, liquid, and solid. Gas and solid are the two extremes because one is without form and the other is a rigidly fixed form. In an ideal relationship, we are more like the liquid state because it allows us the most elasticity. We don't crack from being too fixed, nor do we evaporate. Besides being flexible, water is self-leveling and able to find balance regardless of being bumped, sloshed, or poured into strange shapes. To understand our relationship with flexibility, we must understand what drives the extremes.

Jasmine is exhausted. She serves on her child's school Parent Teacher Organization (PTO), works a full-time job, and helps coach one of her children's soccer teams. Jasmine loves to help out where needed and will usually bend over backwards to accommodate other people. Recently she was asked to volunteer at her church in a community outreach role. Jasmine knows she's maxed out and that her husband has already commented multiple times that Jasmine is stretched too thin, but because she's afraid to say "no," she agrees to take on the volunteer role also. As a result, her husband is frustrated that she will be gone from home yet another night of the week. Jasmine wants to please everyone around her—to the detriment of her most important personal relationship.

The overly compliant person is often driven by the need to be liked and accepted, even at their own expense. They may know what they like and want but dismiss it in the attempt to be liked and accepted. This will present much like the classic codependent who just can't say no to others, including their partner. The problem is that they often become burned out over time, since the more they give, the more others take until they are exhausted and can't give anymore. Sadly, these people will typically lash out or pull away at this point but will later feel bad and the cycle will start over. They are often unable to recognize the cycle and thus are doomed to keep repeating the pattern.

On the other extreme, the overly rigid person is seen as inflexible and fixed in their thinking, position, or approach. It's often "my way or the highway" with them. These people usually have a high need for certainty and control, likely as a response to others having let them down and being undependable. The highly rigid person has concluded that they can't trust others and can only depend on themselves. The views of others may be dismissed, rejected, or disregarded for what they see as the only right answer—theirs. They have already looked at the evidence and have made their decision. People on this extreme might become angry when challenged or questioned and may be considered intolerant. They're even prone to throwing down the gauntlet with ultimatums.

Thomas grew up in a lowly socioeconomic household. He began working straight out of high school and takes pride in the business he grew himself. He has a difficult time delegating work to others and is adamant with his wife that he's in charge of the checkbook. His wife is a very capable woman, but Thomas wants control over their family finances. He openly admits this is because he grew up without means and doesn't want to live that way again. However, his need for that tight control and security makes his wife feel run over at times.

When the two extremes marry, it produces serious challenges—challenges that make processing conflict and growing the relationship much more arduous. To have a healthy relationship with the right balance of flexibility, you'll need to be compromising in how you approach each other with any conflict. There are hills worth dying on, so at times, for your own sake and the sake of your family and relationship, you must take a stand. But not every issue or battle needs to be won at all costs. Sometimes compromise or even retreat is the better part of valor. Knowing when to retreat and when to advance (or dig in) makes all the difference. And sometimes, what looks like rigidity or weakness is misinterpreted. Other times, it's understandable.

Terry insists that they only take their car into a specific repair shop, even though there is a closer one to the house. His wife, Sandra, needs to take the car in for repairs and is frustrated over Terry's inflexibility. Upon investigation, she learned that Terry is simply showing loyalty to an old Army buddy of his, who's a mechanic at that shop. This buddy was there for Terry and Sandra years ago when their youngest child had some health issues. Terry insists that they take the car there so his friend can do the maintenance and get the money. After learning this, Sandra acknowledged that one of Terry's best traits is loyalty, and she understands the situation differently now. Sure, Terry is still being rigid, but Sandra understands and even agrees.

The issue that everyone faces related to flexibility is the internal struggle with their own thoughts, emotions, and will. Simply put, we believe our own unique perspective. Sometimes what appears as being rigid has a legitimate explanation, and it is our responsibility to listen and explain our thinking to our mates.

Why Are We Inflexible?

Our flexibility (and likewise, our rigidities) stem from our perceptions or perspectives. Our perceptions are born of our combined past experiences, unique traits, personal values, and even internal vows. As we travel through life, we take in new information and build our personal storehouse of experiences (learned in the first, second and third person), and we assign them meanings. Sometimes we assign (learn) meaning and value through our own personal experiences; other times, we learn vicariously through others. We don't have to be hit by a speeding car ourselves to learn that when it comes to a car-versus-pedestrian scenario, the car wins.

Have you ever put on someone else's glasses? Whoa! It's disorienting, right? After all, it's not a prescription meant for you. And the same would be true for someone putting on your glasses (if you wear glasses like we do). We each have our own unique prescriptions that we see through. In relationships, we have to learn to see through our mate's prescription glasses and also be able to describe and help them see what we see through our own unique prescription. That's flexibility—the willingness to be open to see and learn.

When we become rigid, we decide that the information we have is correct and there is no other way of looking at it. What needs to change, if hit by a car, so we can feel safe enough to cross that street again, as opposed to just never crossing? Just like your personal prescription will change over time, don't insist that your prescription must also be your mate's prescription. Never mind that one of you is more nearsighted than the other—or that one of you has astigmatism!

Remember that the root word in the word "relationship" is "relate". It means "to establish a connection with". You might even hear us explain it as taking a shot at wearing your partner's prescription. Relationships are about being a witness to the other person's life. That exposure is part of what gives us the ability to grow and thus see the world differently. It's in relationships that we find the greatest potential for growth because we're not just looking at the world through our own lens but also seeing through the lens of another person.

Now, please don't think we're suggesting that relationships are built of one rigid partner and one compliant partner. We have worked with those and with couples where both parties are very rigid, as well as couples where both parties are overly compliant. Not one of these scenarios works.

Our most rigid clients tend to be people that have careers in which they make decisions all day with little or no questioning. They are the expert or lead. We also find rigidity is very common when people have been single for an extended time or get married late in life. This is not always the case, but it is more often than not. And it's understandable, as these people haven't had to be accountable and compromising. They can be set in their ways. Remember the adage, "You can't teach an old dog new tricks?" Well, it has some validity here.

Conditional or inconsistent flexibility can also be a challenge. It is not uncommon for spouses to say that their mate is very rigid about some things or situations and not others—or, only on specific topics.

The happiest couples work to grow their awareness and strike a balance with flexibility. They strive not to be too flexible or too inflexible. They focus more on being happy and less on being right. They avoid absolute, blaming statements like "you always" and "you never" and trade them in for "I" statements that state how they feel. They want to understand and honor their mate's position, which doesn't exclude getting their own needs met. They lovingly learn to ask probing questions and, if needed, call out their mates—again, lovingly, and never in front of others, especially the children.

They are also prone to having systems in place to question each other so they can both communicate effectively and work together towards resolving conflict. This allows people to move past old emotional triggers and limit the impact a conflict might have. This is navigating conflict effectively. When done in a relationship, it builds greater intimacy and connection within a couple.

The Tree Experiment

Somewhere between overly compliant and overly rigid is the sweet spot of flexibility. This is where we want to reside in our relationships.

Several years ago, researchers placed some young trees in a greenhouse. One group was tied to and supported by a stake. A second group was left to grow without stakes. And a third group was not staked but waved back and forth manually for several minutes every day.

At the end of several months, the three groups of trees were measured for growth in height and trunk diameter. The results were interesting. The staked trees were the tallest and weakest (small trunk diameter). The trees with no stakes were intermediate in height and trunk diameter, and many were not growing straight. Surprisingly, the trees that were waved back and forth each day without being staked were the shortest but had the greatest trunk diameter and were thus determined to be the strongest.

Overly rigid individuals are like the first group of trees—staked, firm, and unwavering. They may look tall and capable, but their foundation is weak. Overly compliant individuals are much like the second group of trees—growing aimlessly in unpredictable directions and lacking in strength. Folks who find the sweet spot of flexibility remind us of the third group of trees. They might not look like the tallest and most powerful, but their firm foundations make them the strongest. They are least susceptible to damage from heavy storms.

The Bottom Line

Flexibility is the vehicle that lets you consider another way of looking at things. Again, it's one of the most important elements in this book and is the single biggest hurdle keeping many couples from having their own wildly successful relationship. So, learning about where you lie on the flexibility continuum and the role and impact that it plays in your life and relationship is paramount to the process.

We must gauge where we fall on the flexibility/rigidity spectrum and why we fall there. Awareness of this helps us communicate with our mates and creates the opportunity for better understanding among spouses. It gives us the chance to view life through one another's prescription glasses.

A LOOK IN THE MIRROR

1. Would you describe yourself as rigid, overly compliant, or flexible? What would your mate say you are?

2. How would you describe your mate on the spectrum? How would they describe themselves?

3. In what areas of life are you more rigid or more flexible? Why the difference?

4. Are there areas in life where you notice your mate being more rigid or more flexible? Do you know why they feel differently about those topics?

5. What is the danger to your relationship when being overly rigid?

6. What is the danger to your relationship when being overly flexible?

7. Can you name a time where you chose to be flexible with your mate and it helped you to better understand where they were coming from? How did this grow you as a couple?

GRATITUDE

—

The quality or feeling of being grateful or thankful.

ONE OF OUR FRIENDS IS A PHOTOGRAPHER. WE'VE ALWAYS ADMIRED his creative eye and his ability to capture the perfect moment—to preserve it for always. Our friend and his wife once accompanied us on one of our weekend getaways. We stayed at a cabin in the woods and had a grand time! Throughout the weekend, our friend would be behind his camera capturing photos of his wife, the scenery, and even us. One day we watched him kneeling by a creek, adjusting his lens, and trying to capture a photo of some water running over a rock. When he showed us the photo, we were stunned by its beauty. We had stood by the creek with him and looked at the exact same water. But what he saw (and captured on film) was different from what we saw. Certain aspects of the scenery caught his eye, and he used his camera to focus on those aspects. As he puts it, what he chooses to focus on becomes the subject of the work.

It's true in so many ways, isn't it? What you look for is what you will find. What we focus on, dwell on, and go looking for is what we will see, even to the exclusion of evidence that might prove our preconceived ideas wrong. We dwell on and create momentum in one direction or another.

This is precisely why gratitude is a fundamental element to any successful marriage. Gratitude shifts your focus so that you see the wonderful, the good, the irreplaceable, and the valuable rather than the things of this world that build negativity and discontentment with our mates.

Gratitude is More Than Saying Thanks

Gratitude is about thankfulness and recognizing what is right and well. It is about appreciating what you have while also striving for more. Gratitude fuels joy and contentment.

Gratitude is more than the notion that the glass is half-full. It is an approach to life and happiness. Gratitude is the story of what one focuses on. It's the habit of making the best of any situation and looking for the hidden lessons or takeaways when things go awry.

> Gratitude is more than the notion that the glass is half-full. It is an approach to life and happiness.

We adopted a saying that we use often: "Don't judge something to be a tragedy on the day that it happens. You never know what can come of something and the beauty that can arise from it."

Maybe you've heard the Chinese proverb about a farmer and his son. The farmer's son was trying to break one of their mares, but she threw him to the ground, breaking his leg. Everyone in their village agreed this seemed to be such terrible luck. The farmer was just relieved his son only had a broken leg, and not a broken neck or back.

A few weeks later, soldiers from the national army marched through the village, recruiting all the able-bodied boys for the army. They did not take the farmer's son, who was still recovering from his injury. Everyone in their village agreed this seemed to be fantastic luck. The farmer's son would be safe at home. The farmer was just relieved his son had a broken leg, and therefore would not have to face the cruelty of war and the possibility of death.

The moral of this story is, of course, that life is much more agreeable if we merely accept what we're given and make the best of our life circumstances. The farmer knew if his son had left for war, he might have been killed and never returned. Different circumstances would mean a different outcome.

Appreciation is the Not-So-Secret Secret

Appreciation leads to gratitude for what we have and the resolve to make the best of our circumstances. Your level of gratitude and your gratitude set point dictate your level of happiness. And your perspective becomes your reality. When we change our perspectives, we create the ability to see a new reality. If circumstances were different, we realize, we might just feel differently.

For example, while one woman resents her husband because he won't put his socks in the hamper, another woman is lonely and would love the opportunity to have a husband to fuss over for leaving his socks on the floor. While one husband is frustrated with his wife for the time and attention she spends on the kids, another husband remembers the pain in his wife's eyes the day they buried their little boy. Perspective.

A client might complain that her husband wants to have sex all the time, while another comes in and say, "My husband doesn't find me attractive and won't have sex with me." One wife wants her husband to spend more time with her, and another feels her husband is too needy and should spend more time with his friends. A man might feel overwhelmed at having to help with household maintenance at his elderly parents' home. Another man's eyes fill with tears whenever he drives by his childhood home, which had to be sold when his father died, and his mother went into assisted living. Thankfully, he still gets to see her every Sunday afternoon. Gratitude.

Having an appreciation for even the frustrating things and being able to put things in perspective is huge. And transformative. And humbling. It is the ability to make molehills out of mountains, rather than mountains out of molehills. It's the realization that no matter what your circumstances are, it could be worse.

Gratitude Impacts Your Life and Marriage

Maybe you are familiar with the story, "Two Wolves," a popular Cherokee legend that is also known as "Which One Do You Feed?" In the story, a grandfather explains inner conflicts to his grandson by using the metaphor of two wolves (one black and one white) fighting within him. When his grandson asks which wolf wins, the grandfather answers that whichever he chooses to feed is the one that wins.

This sets the tone for what we feed and focus on in marriage. If you keep feeding the black wolf, then you have what the black wolf brings. If you choose to feed the white wolf, you have what the white wolf brings. Gratitude is feeding the wolf that is optimistic, appreciative, and supportive. Gratitude is keeping the pessimistic, needy wolf at bay, while realizing that he is still there, waiting to intrude. Gratitude helps maintain your focus. You have the choice to feel gratitude today and every day. Don't let the opportunity pass you by.

The Time for Gratitude is Now

Let us tell you about John and Sandra. While alive, John worked long hours and strived for his family, yet his wife Sandra never seemed grateful. There was always more to do, and things were rarely done right. He died unexpectedly after 30 years of marriage; and now, Sandra has canonized him. Her gratitude is abundant for what he brought to the table, and she recounts stories of home improvements that he did, his work ethic, his love for his kids, and his friendships. She goes on and on. Yet, when he was alive, she showed little gratitude for him.

The time for gratitude is today and every day. We know your mate is not perfect. No one is. But that shouldn't stop you from looking for and expressing gratitude.

Dr. Leo Buscaglia believed that we should live life in a way that we are never "waiting for tomorrow." He stated, "We don't know what might happen in the very next moment, and that moment may be lost forever."

In his book, *Loving, Living, & Learning*, Professor Buscaglia explained his feelings about "putting off and putting off and putting off" by using a moving poem by an unknown female student that he had found on his desk after one of his classes:

"Things You Didn't Do"
Author Unknown

Remember the day I borrowed your brand-new car and I dented it?
I thought you'd kill me, but you didn't.
And remember the time I dragged you to the beach, and you said it would rain, and it did?
I thought you'd say, "I told you so." But you didn't.
Do you remember the time I flirted with all the guys to make you jealous, and you were?
I thought you'd leave me, but you didn't.
Do you remember the time I spilled strawberry pie all over your car rug?
I thought you'd hit me, but you didn't.
And remember the time I forgot to tell you the dance was formal, and you showed up in jeans?
I thought you'd drop me, but you didn't.
Yes, there were lots of things you didn't do.
But you put up with me, and you loved me, and you protected me.
There were lots of things I wanted to make up to you when you returned from Vietnam.
But you didn't.

As Buscaglia's student teaches us all, the time to "do" that nice thing you want to do is now!

Comparison Has Consequences

Comparing your mate to others is the opposite of gratitude and appreciation. And it is destructive. Each of us has a unique set of abilities and skills, and we all have deficits and weaknesses. It's what we do with each of these and the weight or emphasis that we assign to them that makes the difference. Remember—which wolf are you feeding?

If you follow our blogs, you may have read our posts about comparisons. In it, we write about how comparisons can kill the intimacy in your relationship and lead to feelings of inadequacy, discouragement, or even humiliation. And not just on the part of the spouse being evaluated—such comparisons can affect both of you negatively. You may begin to harbor resentment if you only focus on the things your spouse does that annoy you. Instead, try to focus more on what they get right. By focusing on the positive, we can nurture and grow the positive in our relationships.

When we compare our mates to another, we can be prone to critique them, and no one likes to be under the microscope of criticism. Too often, we focus on something that's different and label it as wrong. Different does not equal wrong. In fact, different can actually be better. We are repeatedly reminded of this within our own marriage and with our clients.

But let's be honest, gratitude is a Catch-22 situation. It is difficult to be grateful about something without comparing it to how or what things could be otherwise. And when we are grateful, it's because we're not looking at what could be bad or wrong.

This is much like climbing a mountain. You might tend to look ahead and see how far you still have to go, but you should also look back and see just how far you've come. It's a delicate balance—but doable—to be striving forward while also tracking your progress. Gratitude lies in the wisdom of realizing what you have and how far you've come while also understanding that growth and opportunity are always before us.

Maintaining gratitude means that our approach to disagreements, differences, and challenges must be done with wisdom, compassion, and understanding: wisdom from the past, compassion for each person, and understanding that you will both get it wrong sometimes and right sometimes. **C is for Conflict** teaches us the ways to resolve conflict and to understand that conflict is a natural part of a relationship—not to be feared, but to be embrac^ed and navigated with gusto.

Gratitude is being appreciative when your mate brings you flowers, even if it is not your favorite type. Maybe the store was out of your favorite. Maybe your favorite looked wilted and old. Or maybe your mate wanted to switch things up a bit. Hey, they bought you flowers! They spent money and invested time and energy to try and make you smile, and that should count—a lot. Gratitude is appreciating where your mate's skill set is strong, rather than focusing on where they are not as strong, and vice-versa.

Techniques for Growing Gratitude in Life and Marriage

I (Kimberly) love assigning Relationship Reverse Bucket Lists (RR-BLs) activities to couples. A reverse bucket list is where you look back on what's already been accomplished and experienced rather than listing all the things that haven't yet been done.

What is your mate amazing at? What ways has your mate served and loved you? How has your mate (and marriage) grown? What have you and your mate conquered in your marriage? Recount these items on an RRBL instead of focusing on everything you haven't done or conquered yet.

Also, consider something great about your partner alphabetically; for example, A is for Active with Kids, and B is for Brave. You get the idea. These may seem like simple activities, but they can be transformative for your mate, who will see what you appreciate about them. It will also help you with your mindset. Again, what you look for, you find.

Never underestimate the power of a gratitude journal (GJ). Here is a secret. The richest value of a gratitude journal is not in the moment of writing down what you're grateful for. The power lies in the area that is most often underutilized—rereading it! Yes, rereading it. When times are tough or you are struggling, go back and read your gratitude journal or your Relationship Reverse Bucket List (RRBL). That's when you most need it.

A set point is a position you habitually fall into, whether it's happiness, weight, etc. In relationships, it is crucial for you to not only be aware of your set point but to actively do things regularly to move the needle in the right direction. Rereading your GJ and your RRBL are valuable in this area.

Interestingly, we humans are rarely at our best when we are stagnant or complacent, which commonly results in focusing on the negative or becoming hyper self-centered. That's why there is not only value in couples striving together, but also in consciously making sure, with sustained effort, that gratitude is a cornerstone of their relationship.

When clients say that they just fell out of love, it is often simply the complacency and apathy that stems from a lack of engagement as well as a lack of gratitude.

The Bottom Line

Gratitude drives your happiness and set points. It is important that we not focus on what we didn't get, but rather on what we have. Look at your elderly family members and neighbors. You can easily recognize those who have gratitude for life and all their life experiences, even those who have faced significant heartaches and tragedies.

Gratitude impacts your ability to forgive, recover, and live a balanced life. It is a mindset. Some people can have all they ever wanted and are still not happy or grateful.

You are in control of your gratitude. You have control over what you choose, what you focus on, what you think about, and to a degree, the importance you place on things. What is the story that you tell yourself? What do you take from your experiences? As human beings, we seek to make meaning, to reconcile and learn from our experiences. Gratitude is the key to making positive meaning out of experiences and life.

If you are lucky, you will have a time of reflection at the end of your life—the good, the bad, and the undetermined. Whether or not it's a successful life, avoid being bitter and reflect with perspective about your time on earth. It's a wondrous gift. Practicing gratitude now ensures that when your life is remembered, either by you or whoever gives your eulogy, it will be done with positivity and grace.

A LOOK IN THE MIRROR

1. Which "wolf" do you feed—discontentment or gratitude?

2. Name three things you appreciate about your mate.

3. How can you better express your gratitude for your mate?

4. How would you like your mate to express gratitude towards you?

5. Can you think of a time when you chose to compare instead of being grateful? What happened? What could you have done differently?

6. Can you think of a painful or difficult season that taught you gratitude?

7. Do the ABCs of gratitude for your mate. Leave sticky notes around the house for your mate until they find all 26 alphabetical pieces of gratitude.

HOPE

—

A desire accompanied by an expectation or belief that it will be fulfilled.

THERE IS AN ADAGE THAT SAYS WE CAN GO FOUR WEEKS WITHOUT food, four days without water, four minutes without air, and only four seconds without hope. Others might use the rule of 3s, where we can go three weeks without food, three days without water, three minutes without air, and only three seconds without hope. Whichever you use (and without a big math or science argument), the wisdom that is conveyed is the same—hope is crucial to our survival.

What is hope? Is it head-in-the-sand, ignoring all the warning signs? Is it unwavering faith in yourself and your mate? Is it based on your beliefs about life, love, and marriage? Or is it to keep moving and believing, like in the country song *If You're Going through Hell* by Rodney Atkins?

> *If you're goin' through hell, keep on going*
> *Don't slow down, if you're scared, don't show it*
> *You might get out before the devil even knows you're there*

Hope vs. Faith

Hope is generally considered a positive mental state or expectation about future events or people. Hope is the idea that something will succeed, or an outcome will be as expected. Faith, however, is unwavering *trust* and confidence in something or someone. It is a result of your current belief systems as shaped by experiences.

Is it possible to have hope without faith? We argue, "No. Hope and faith are intimately connected." The Bible tells us in Hebrews 11:1, *"Now faith is the substance of things hoped for, the evidence of things not seen."* KJV

Is your idea of hope really a faith that if you don't do anything at all, it will all work out anyway? Or is it more akin to your belief in a better future because you believe in yourself and your partner?

When we get to element **T**, we will discuss trust, but for now, we'll just say that trust is hope in someone or something else. Do you trust that your spouse is working late when they say they are? Or do you just hope they are? Do you have faith in their word? Is it possible to have faith without trust? Again, we argue no. But more on that later.

Hope Can Save

Injecting hope is the single most important thing in saving a troubled marriage. In marriage counseling and mentoring, the first task is to instill hope. If your partner feels hopeless or that there is no pathway to success, then getting even the smallest dose of hope is crucial. Hope is the antidote to apathy and can start with a single act: a single act by either you or your partner. So don't be afraid to be the one to make the small steps to instill hope.

Sizing up the situation to determine the level of hope starts with assessing if people are willing to put in the effort, even if minimal, to regain hope. Your job as a mate is to give your partner a reason to keep hoping and keep the relationship alive, and to avoid words and actions that will diminish their hope.

We have an exercise that we assign clients to get hope back on track. It is a small token and a great starting place for many couples. It begins with each partner sharing one small thing that their partner could do for them daily for a week that would make them feel loved and heard. It might be sending a mid-day text to say "hello" or "I am thinking of you." Or asking at the end of the day how their day was. Leaving them a note. Bringing a flower. Sitting and having coffee or breakfast. Making the bed. Folding the laundry. Putting your shoes up. Making toast in the morning. Putting gas in the car. You get the idea.

Hope Buys You Time to Decide

In the midst of hopelessness and despair, even limited and misplaced hope has value. It can allot you time to think, wisdom, and the ability to see things more clearly. Hope can also be a form of communication with your mate. For example, when one mate is experiencing betrayal by their partner, they can communicate the level of hope as limited or minimal. In the case of our clients, this usually means that they desire to have hope but feel considerably less hope than before. It can be helpful to assess the level of hope on a scale of 1 to 10.

What is your current level of hope and why? Are you increasing the level of hope, or are you stuck at a level? If you're at least moving in a positive direction, even by very small increments, the pace or rate of change is less concerning because you'll gain momentum as you go. If you're moving in a negative direction, however, we're very concerned about the speed of movement. Are you in a downward spiral that is going to be almost impossible to pull out of? Are you at a point of no return? Or is this more a hiccup or turbulence?

When we ask our clients to tell us about their level of hope, we ask them to consider these categories: certain hope, unwavering hope, reasonable hope, realistic hope, questionable hope, minimal hope, and misplaced hope (which some even label as false hope). There are varying levels of hope. Where are you?

Hopelessness and Its Effects

There are seasons in life that can have a negative impact or at least make it more likely to have a negative impact on our level of hope. These seasons can be predictable, like empty nesting, or can come out of no-where, like a serious, unexpected illness or the loss of a child. Some seasons, like the birth of a child, can cause unexpected impacts like postpartum depression at a time when you are expecting to feel only joy. These seasons affect you as a couple, even if you consider it more of a personal season experienced by only one of the spouses.

Personal trials and seasons can result from lack of hope and, when coupled with a lack of engagement, can result in a sense of fatalism. One or both spouses can feel that any effort is futile. It is human nature to want to feel a sense of control or efficacy in producing a desired outcome. And, in a search for control when a person feels they have none, they can turn to sabotage.

Sabotage gives people a feeling that at least they can control failure. When clients report they are "just tired," we ask, "Tired of what? Tired of having no impact or effect? Tired of putting in effort with no hope of a positive return? Tired of feeling like you have no control, perhaps?"

It is important to recognize that effort is required in all options. Effort is needed to rebuild the relationship, and effort is also required to build a whole new life—one that does not include your spouse in an intimate relationship. Hope is what helps us keep looking forward to a positive outcome, but change is the action necessary to achieving it. As you face any challenge in your relationship, remember that the only constant in life is change.

Reinstituting Hope

Yes, hope stems from a feeling of efficacy and control, but it also pulls from a sense of gratitude.

Gratitude in one area of our lives can bleed into other areas to help us feel more grateful overall. If you are struggling in your relationship, try focusing on gratitude or better yet, reading the **G is for Gratitude** element. Make a concerted effort to look for things to be grateful for. We are not normally fans of "at least" statements, but sometimes they are just the ticket to restore hope. These remind us of the adage of the man who said, "I cried because I had no shoes, but then I saw a man with no feet." There is almost always something positive on which to focus.

True, it is much like a consolation prize, but recognizing that it could be worse can sometimes help us not to dwell on the severity of the situation.

An often-overlooked impact of a lack or loss of hope is that it erodes our sense of identity. When we lose hope about our own sense of identity, *who we are, what we are,* and *where we are going* comes into question. Lack of hope seeps into the rest of our lives. It piggybacks our worldviews and can create an existential crisis.

It is entirely acceptable to keep fighting for your marriage even when you have a lack of hope that it will get better, even if the sole purpose of doing it is for the children. Yes, we just said that! Statistics actually indicate that when folks stick with a marriage, provided there is no abuse, the marriage can heal itself like a bodily wound does.

Take the liver, for example. The liver is a unique organ. It's the only organ in the body that can regenerate. With most organs, such as the heart, the damaged tissue is replaced with a scar, just like on the skin. The liver, however, can replace its damaged tissue with new cells. There are documented cases of extreme liver damage in which up to 60% of liver cells were killed within just a few days by something like an acetaminophen overdose, and, when there was no reinjury, the liver was already repairing itself after 6 weeks. Think about how miraculous that is! Simply by ceasing harm to the liver, one can rejuvenate and heal it until it's fully functional. Imagine having hope that our relationships can do the same thing if we just stop injuring them.

We must remember that where our intimate emotions are concerned (love, hate, joy, grief), no amount of healing can occur by just ignoring those emotions or giving them space. We must have hope, and remember that in most instances, the best way to deal with the chaos in life is to confront it. The very first step to healing is to NOT do more damage. And that's a good first step. Preventing further damage to our relationships often gives us enough stability to begin to heal, just as in the case of the liver.

Statistics also indicate that upwards of 50% of divorced people regret their divorce. You may not be able to control your partner, but you can control yourself; and with hope, you will often affect your partner in a positive way.

Hope Leads to Surviving and Thriving

In the book, *Man's Search for Meaning*, by Viktor Frankl, the author reports that many of the survivors of the German concentration camps reported surviving because they had something to come back to. They had hope. Hope that there was something on the other side of all their struggles and pain.

Relationship expert Esther Perel, whose parents were in concentration camps, recounts a similar observation from the people that were liberated from concentration camps. She shares that there were those that "didn't die" and those that "came back to life". She writes of her parents, "They came out of that experience wanting to charge at life with a vengeance and to make the most of each day. They both felt that they had been granted a unique gift: living life again. My parents didn't just want to survive, they wanted to revive." In her practice, she places emphasis on the difference between "not being dead" and "being alive".

Some fellow prisoners in those concentration camps chided the ones with hope. This is much like folks laughing at someone with hope who is trying to hold on to a troubled marriage. People might call you a sucker or even cajole you into leaving your mate by saying things like, "I would never put up with that." But those with hope don't succumb to the chiding of others.

The Bottom Line

Hope waxes and wanes and ebbs and flows in marriages and life in general. This is natural. Events, seasons in the year, other stressors, etc., can and will impact your level of hope. Recognize that many of these hope debasers are fleeting or temporary. Don't make long-term or permanent decisions based on these temporary events.

Hope allows us to persevere. It affords us time and patience, and it can displace negative events and circumstances in life—but only if we let it. Don't let one day of hopelessness become a week's or a month's or a year's worth.

> Hope is gratitude for the future, for the seasons in life, in marriage, and in future anticipation of being grateful.

Hopelessness: it's a serious situation! Hopelessness causes people to take drastic measures. A lack of hope sets up a cascade of other things, feelings, and events. Take a course of action to regain your hope.

Hope is willingness to change. Hope is a partner who has positive intentions. One person in a marriage can change its course for the better—or for worse. Hope is what helps us navigate and look forward. Hope is gratitude for the future, for the seasons in life, in marriage, and in future anticipation of being grateful.

Hope is an unlimited resource. It is boundless. One just has to look for it and take small actions to nurture it. Small actions like reading this book; giving a token of love; focusing on gratitude; and actively seeking hope.

A LOOK IN THE MIRROR

1. What things do you hope for in life?

2. What hopes do you have for your marriage?

3. What is your current level of hope and why?

4. In what ways are you feeding hope towards your mate?

5. Have you ever faced a difficult season and clung to hope as you journeyed through it?

6. How have you seen someone's hopelessness lead to more pain?

7. What is one small action you can take today to grow hope in yourself and for others?

INTIMACY

The emotional and spiritual union between two people.

ARE YOU A BIG SALT LOVER? DO YOU SPRINKLE SOME ON EVERY-thing? Salt is a chemical compound called sodium chloride, and it's created when the elements sodium (Na) and chloride (Cl) are joined. (Chemistry experts, please forgive us for oversimplifying.)

Sodium chloride (salt) is one of the most abundant compounds in the world and a very necessary one at that. Salt also is a wonderful preservative and a great way to add flavor to otherwise bland food. It's not only beneficial but necessary. Every human being needs some amount of salt. Salt helps balance fluids in the body and maintain a healthy blood pressure. It's crucial for healthy nerve and muscle function, too.

On their own, both sodium and chloride have a very different purpose; but when joined together, they make something new and wonderful.

This is much like what happens in a couple. As individuals, you are great people. But, when you join together intimately, you create something that gives you a healthy marriage and adds delicious flavor to your lives!

So Much More Than Sex

When people think of intimacy, they tend to immediately leap to the topic of sex. Yes, sex is an act of intimacy. But intimacy is more than the physical coupling of two individuals. It's the coupling of two souls. Intimacy is probably one of the most misunderstood words in relationship dynamics. The areas dedicated to intimacy in bookstores prove that it is a sought-after subject. Yet, it remains an elusive concept left to romance novels, greeting cards, and Hallmark movies.

Is it just a feeling we have? Or is it a state of being we can achieve if we meet the "right" person or have the same things in common? Is it a stage or level we can obtain if we follow the right steps and do and say just the right things? Is it a place we can only visit and are not allowed to stay? Does it only happen if all the stars are aligned in the right order?

What is intimacy? Why are so many people in search of it while so few seem to be able to achieve it? With the divorce rate holding at just under 50% and affairs at an all-time high, why have we not been able to crack the code on the mystery of intimacy? The short answer is that people don't know how.

The longer and more complicated answer: almost nobody wants to go where they need to go in order to achieve it. Carl Jung, the father of analytical psychology, probably says it best: "That which you most need will be found where you least want to look!"

Sue Johnson, a researcher, clinical psychologist, and the author of the *Hold Me Tight* book, felt that for years, intimacy was not quite understood by couples. In her book, she demystifies some of the confusion surrounding what intimacy is and is not by saying that the key to relationship intimacy comes through relating with and attuning to our mates. (Side note: Most of her approach is based in attachment theory, but we suggest that if you're seeking counseling help for intimacy, work with a therapist experienced in EFT—Emotionally Focused Therapy.)

Facing Your Dragon(s)

Developing intimacy is analogous to the mythological story of the dragon and the gold he protects. The path to the gold (the object of our desires) always has a dragon guarding it. If you want the gold, you must not only face the dragon but also defeat it.

Nothing of value comes easy. If it did, it would cease to have much worth. This is true with intimacy. Everyone wants it, but few are willing to face their dragon(s) to obtain that which they desire. Intimacy is not found in the safe places of calm, tranquil waters. No, it's found in raging waters, at the edge of steep cliffs, and in dark, damp places, and that's where your own dragon lives.

If you're not willing to go to the emotional places you least want to go to, chances are that you're probably not up for a trip to the dragon's lair and the treasure to be found there.

Intimacy is the combination of three things: vulnerability, transparency, and authenticity. It also requires the ability to be comfortable with a certain level of emotional discomfort or tension. Further, it is the culmination of several of the elements discussed in this book, which work together much like a series of lenses coming into focus.

You can't achieve intimacy by just doing things "right" or checking a list called, "Just Do These 10 Things." Rather, it's an individual journey of you and your mate, separately and together, over a period of time, that results in mutual discovery and depth.

The past few years have seen a lot of research surface on the area of intimacy. It all seems to boil down to attuning to one another and accepting each other's differences—including being willing to see things differently than your partner and tolerating one another while also being authentic and transparent with each other.

The challenge is that too many people don't understand their own emotions, let alone articulate them in a way that their partner can understand. Interestingly, people will be more authentic and vulnerable with a stranger than they will with a person they feel could reject them. For many, it's the death of a thousand cuts (from real or imagined hurts) that keeps us from risking and achieving emotional intimacy. This fear of rejection is our dreaded dragon. To get the gold, one needs to first defeat or at least face (perhaps even befriend) their emotional dragons. Sadly, there are many dragons—and some even magically come back to life and have to be slain over and over again.

What Are Your Dragons?

Do you have a strong need to feel respected or cherished, resulting in a lack of willingness to be seen as "less than" by your partner? Does a low self-image propel you to do for others to win love and acceptance? Maybe your dragon lies in your past, where people have repeatedly let you down and hurt you, causing a lack of trust that keeps you from ever approaching the cave to face the intimacy dragon again.

Facing the dragon (your fears) means taking risks. And even though you know that the bounty is there (perhaps you can even see the jewels and gold reflecting and shining), your fears make the risk too great to seek the potential reward. You resign yourself by saying, "I don't really want the gold and jewels anyway."

People may want the reward of intimacy, but they are not willing to be seen authentically enough to let go of the facade they have built. The facade has been the focus or distraction from intimacy. Your facade has been built and reinforced over time, and it has seemingly served you well. Or has it? It's kept you from reaching the bounty—the reward of intimacy. Does it really provide a service? Or a hindrance?

People naturally look to others for meaning and purpose but are prone to giving away their own personal power in search of love. Or lack of trust keeps them from ever drawing close to others. Neither of these will get you the reward of true intimacy.

Intimacy is found when, despite the dreaded dragon, you accept the risk of fully knowing your partner and allowing yourself to be fully known. This is not a switch that one just turns on. It takes time. It takes practice. It is a process of repeated confrontation, slaying the dragon over and over. The good thing is that it gets easier (hope that helps)! Just like we talk about in other elements in this book, it's about being comfortable with being uncomfortable. You will find a complementary description in **V is for Vulnerability**.

There are plenty of justifications that keep people from opening up emotionally and reaching the intimacy they desire. Some are excuses; others are fears. Some seem reasonable, and others irrational. Nevertheless, they're the barriers preventing you from the bounty that is only found in true intimacy.

Don't Be Afraid

Sadly, a fear of intimacy is highly contagious and can be caught by and from our partner, our children, and other people with whom we come into contact. What did your parents teach you about intimacy? That it's something to be feared and avoided, or something to be sought after with gusto? Or is it somewhere in between? Do your religious beliefs impact your views on intimacy? What are you teaching those around you? Sadly, even the media influences our willingness to seek intimacy. TV shows and "influencers" have multiple marriages, and they glamorize affairs, downplay commitment, and emphasize a "what's-in-it for-me?" type of attitude. Authenticity and transparency aren't exactly glamorized.

The often-repeated statistic that 50% of marriages fail can hinder our willingness to embrace intimacy and vulnerability. After all, what's the point of facing that dragon if you're bound to lose? Unless, of course, you're the rebel type who raises your hand and says, "I'm going to be in the 50% that succeeds! I'm going to face that dragon, look him in the eye, stare him down, and take back my power! In fact, I'm going to befriend him after I beat him and thank him for his service as I move past him to my reward."

It Carries Into the Bedroom

Lack of intimacy is widespread. It metastasizes as it spreads from our minds to our hearts to our bedrooms. With so many negative inputs to discourage us from intimacy and vulnerability, it is no wonder that so many couples struggle with sexuality. Struggles in the bedroom are directly connected to struggles with vulnerability, and struggles with vulnerability hinder intimacy.

It is very commonplace for couples in counseling to report sexual issues. In the vast majority of cases, however, it's not actually a sexual issue. It's an intimacy issue. Emotional intimacy is the fuel that drives effective sexual intimacy. And without the protection of emotional intimacy, couples have trouble finding the gold and jewels in their relationship.

We've worked with countless couples to help them walk to this point of the cave and to understand the techniques and mindset it takes to defeat the dragon. We understand that it can be a haltingly scary place to be. And it requires both willingness and action. It requires a deep awareness and acceptance of oneself, including an acceptance of your own flaws, failures, and limitations, as well as your mate's. It demands that you see your mate's perspectives, not as you think they should be, but as they see them. It also requires you to trust, forgive, and accept. These, along with transparency and authenticity, are the keys to getting past the dragon. Yes, it's often messy and scary in the dragon's cave, but love tends to be that way.

It Takes Two

For a couple to enjoy the intimacy awaiting them, both partners have to be actively pursuing it. It comes with fully knowing your mate and being fully known in return. We commonly meet couples in which one partner seems perfectly content for things to stay as they are while the other one wants "more" from their mate—they want a deeper connection, more communication, and to "feel closer" to their mate.

Unless you both desire this, it won't come. It takes both mates being willing to explore, share, and understand themselves and their mates for intimacy to grow. If you find that you're pushing and prodding your mate about intimacy, we encourage you to examine your methods and approach. While your motives and desires are admirable, you may have to take a different approach to get your desired result.

You have to let your mate know what intimacy is to you, why you want it so badly, and that (here's the biggest piece) you want to do the work before they have to choose whether to join you in the journey. Yes, over time in a marriage, some couples may already have healthy practices in place that grow intimacy. That's awesome! But others may have to intentionally put them in place.

> Carve out regular times to talk with your mate about things other than the day-to-day business of work, household chores, and children.

Intentional efforts toward intimacy include a plethora of small choices and actions. First, just as you make the daily choice to commit to your mate, make a daily choice to grow in intimacy. Carve out regular times to talk with your mate about things other than the day-to-day business of work, household chores, and children. Ask about their hopes, dreams, feelings, etc. This doesn't have to be as awkward as it sounds. It can come with as simple a question as, "Why?" or, "How did that feel?" Stick with it. Let your mate open up. And actually listen.

Both mates have to feel that they are safe to talk, share, and be vulnerable. Knowing our mate's vulnerabilities helps us orchestrate a safe environment for such conversations. Ladies, we're going to let you in on a secret about men and intimacy: Men often struggle with being seen as "less than". So, if he interprets something you say as criticism or judgment (even if you didn't mean it that way), he's going to have a hard time with intimacy. This means that you ladies have to know your men well and show caution in your responses to his efforts.

Remember, working toward intimacy is just that—work. And sometimes that work includes you taking baby steps with your mate as they get more comfortable being open and vulnerable with you.

A Word of Warning

The couple who shares true intimacy is a fortunate couple. What they share is desired by many but obtained by few. They hold the treasure.

So, if that intimacy is damaged due to a significant betrayal such as an affair, it's a different level of pain and heartache. Fear of this pain hinders some from being brave enough to pursue intimacy. But, as painful as the betrayal of an affair can be, couples who survive them say that they were the best worst thing that ever happened to their relationship. While no one wanted or enjoyed the damage to their relationship, the couples who are able to reconcile (and yes, many can be saved) report the affair as a pivotal moment in their marriage that put them on a new path (through the healing) toward an intimacy that they didn't know before.

Guard your intimacy like that dragon guarded your treasure (except better). Guard your heart, guard your mate, guard your marriage. And fight to regain your intimacy if it has been damaged. There is hope for a marriage in the aftermath of a betrayal and those who have survived it can attest to the importance of protecting the treasures they fought so hard to regain.

The Bottom Line

Intimacy is so much more than sex. Yes, it affects what happens in the bedroom, but begins long before you open the bedroom door. Intimacy is a beautiful and priceless state to reach in your marriage, but getting there is a journey of deeper work, vulnerability, and honesty (with you and your mate).

Because intimacy requires us to dive into our views, feelings, hurts, wants, and needs, we may end up discovering something about ourselves that's difficult to face. This is when so many couples quit in the pursuit of intimacy and thus rob themselves and their mates of one of the crucial elements of a wildly successful marriage. The pursuit of intimacy is continual as couples grow individually, go through seasons, and grow as a couple. Be brave, face the dragons, and earn your treasure. And then, do it again! Our pursuit of the treasure that is intimacy is a continual one. It's not a one and done thing, but instead a daily choice as we go through the various seasons in both life and marriage.

A LOOK IN THE MIRROR

1. On a scale of 1 to 10, how would you rate your emotional intimacy with your mate? Ask your mate how they would rate it also. The difference in your perceptions may be intriguing.

2. Which of you two is more likely to pursue the activities that nurture intimacy?

3. What would you say is the biggest obstacle to intimacy in your marriage?

4. What would your mate say is the biggest obstacle?

5. Who or what has played into your views of what intimacy is and what it should be?

6. What dragon(s) must you and your mate face as individuals and as a couple in order to enjoy the treasures that come with intimacy?

7. Can you name a time in your marriage when you noticed that your emotional connection with your mate impacted your sex life, in either a good or bad way?

JOINING

Coming together; becoming a cohesive unit;
working collaboratively and collectively.

IT SEEMS THAT DANCING SHOWS HAVE BECOME A REGULAR PART OF prime-time networks. We must admit —we're impressed by what contestants on shows like *Dancing with the Stars* can do when they work together. The art of dancing involves two separate bodies that move and flow as one. Where one goes, the other goes also. When one needs support or balance, the other provides it. Their hands come together when needed, and their feet move in step with one another. Their movement is so perfectly synchronized that they almost make it look natural. They complement each other.

> Joining is and should be at the heart of why you're in a relationship.

There are many things in life that require the act of joining together to be successful. The most important of these things is a marriage. Joining is the coming together and aligning with your partner on matters between family, friends, and others. It's working collaboratively and collectively. It's being a cohesive unit rather than being divided and possibly at odds.

Joining is and should be at the heart of why you're in a relationship. It's not about either one of you, nor your friends and/or family of origin. It's about the life you make as a couple and how together, as a couple, you face and relate to everybody else. It underpins commitment, trust, intimacy, hope, and beliefs. And thus, it impacts the success of your relationship.

Cleave, Leave and Cleave

Most people have probably learned the word "cleave" from the Bible, in which it means to stick together and/or create a marital bond as in: "cleave to your wife." But depending on how you use that word, it can have the opposite meaning, to cut or sever.

"Cleave," when it means "to cling to or adhere," comes from an Old English word. "Cleave," with the contrary meaning "to split or sever (something)," as you might do with a meat cleaver, also comes from an Old English word, albeit a different one. To avoid confusion, we'll use the word "cleave" to mean "joining."

Joining with your mate is a two-step process including (1) effectively leaving the priorities you had in your single life, even possibly cutting some old relationships such as with old lovers or naysayers and (2) cleaving or adhering to your mate—with commitment. Without taking the first steps of leaving and cleaving, how can you realign your loyalty to your mate above others?

The Choice to Sever Old Ties

Let's be clear that severing old ties and priorities does not mean to cut off all contact with family, friends, and interests.

Typically, when you hear about leaving and cleaving, the term is applied to immediate family members, usually parents. Maintaining a dependence on parents or letting parents have undue influence can spell doom for a fledgling marriage.

Overly involved parents usually provide some sort of assistance—money, advice, employment, connections, social status, family wealth, or things like free childcare or housing. It may seem innocent enough at the time, but it can spell trouble around the corner because there are nearly always strings attached. The giver gives in order to impact outcomes or expects to be able to exercise (at least some) control. While this is often presented as one spouse's parent "just being helpful," this helpfulness can often be seen by the other spouse as manipulative and leave them feeling like they've married not just their partner, but their partner's parent(s) as well. While one spouse may feel controlled and manipulated, the other one only sees the good. The common defensive phrase goes something like this: "Mom is only trying to help—I don't see what the big deal is."

Cleaving and leaving directly correlates with several other elements in this book, including loyalty, awareness, trust, conflict, and flexibility. Seeking parental approval or advice when you should be consulting with your mate is anti-joining and represents weak boundaries.

There are other truly necessary forms of leaving and cleaving; for example, one needs to sever ties with former romantic relationships. It is surprising the number of people who get married while still having some emotional attachment with past loves, preventing them from fully joining with their partners. People must also release past hurts instead of bringing them into their marriages, where it will make joining even more difficult. We know—it is so easy to write, but hard to do.

It's also critical to let go of fears, comparisons, and limiting beliefs about life and love, as well as any former preconceptions about the future, to be able to fully join your mate. Comparing your mate to others—a celebrity, a neighbor, or especially a parent or ex—is equivalent to being tethered to another. In these situations, you might feel torn and confused. Premarital counseling can help in these areas, and post marital counseling can, too.

Cleaving as a Couple

Now, when you hear the words, "leave and cleave," you'll know how important it is to emerge from the past so you can join and cleave together as a couple. Your two families now become three: his, hers, and ours. The failure to leave the old and cleave to the new family you're forming can have unintended results for your relationship, even in unexpected places. Friends (on social media and in person) and other outside influences, such as church, can also inhibit joining.

You might want to refer to **W is for Wise Counsel** to get a better perspective on this. We've seen a lot of negative involvement in which friends and even church members and their leaders inject themselves into people's lives in a very unhealthy, destructive way.

Likewise, a friend, co-worker, or even therapist who tells you what you must do or not do could be creating a wedge in your joining. It's one thing for friends to come alongside you to lend an ear or support, but even they should not try to control or influence you. You also may need to look at **S is for Safety** to evaluate whether you're in a safe relationship.

When outside influences such as friends, families, exes, co-workers, or other relationships come between couples, it can have catastrophic results. It may even prevent a couple from establishing or maintaining that initial trust and makes authentic joining almost impossible. If there was joining but it was weak (or worse, degraded over time), then trust can be eroded and replaced with resentment and anger. When one partner feels the other has sided or keeps siding with others over them, it can create deep-seated resentment. If left unresolved, it can halt any chance of true intimacy and loyalty.

The Daily Choice to Cleave to Your Mate

Deciding to be joined to your mate was not a decision you made on just your wedding day. Yes, you took vows to be joined together in marriage, but it doesn't end there.

Being joined to your mate is a daily choice you must make each morning when you wake. It means choosing, above all feelings and circumstances, to prioritize and pursue your mate and your marriage. It means choosing to be in control of your emotions. It means choosing to resist the temptation to look outside of the marriage for areas of fulfillment that should only come from your mate.

It means continuing to romance your mate even after you've won their heart. It means coming home to dinner from work because your spouse is waiting there for you—the work will always be there to do later. It means putting down your cell phones and talking to the real-life person who is your spouse rather than your followers on social media. Sometimes it means not getting your way because your mate (and ultimately, your marriage) has other needs.

A Note for Parents

Many well-intentioned parents damage their marriages by misplacing priorities. We see this a lot in mothers. A happy young husband and wife may start to feel resentment when children come along and take their place in the relationship. And far too many older couples who become empty nesters look at each other and almost don't recognize one another. They spent years focusing on the kids, and now when the kids are gone, they're left with a stranger as a spouse.

It's understandable that a newborn or young child is going to need a great deal of attention and tending to. They have physical and developmental needs that you—as a parent—must meet. But we must not forget that our mate needs us to be available, too.

Youth sporting events, extracurriculars, and the many other demands of time can have some parents in survival mode. Their kids become their lives. Their schedule, energy, and time revolve solely around their children.

The single greatest thing you can do as a parent to ensure the happy and healthy development of your child is to show them that you love your mate and place priority on your marriage. While children (by nature) will seek to monopolize our time and attention, we must show them that our mates come first. It's not a selfish move by parents, but rather a selfless one of creating a level of safety and security that the children desperately need.

If your child has to participate in one less activity in order to create time for a weekly date night with your mate, then so be it. Part of joining with your mate is remembering that the person you created these beautiful little time suckers with also needs your time, love, and attention. We have to pour into our mates and marriages just as much (if not more) than we do into our kiddos.

Blended Not Stirred

Blended families walk a very thin line related to leaving, cleaving, and weaving together a new family unit. That's one of the primary causes that the failure rate of blended families is so much greater than that of first marriages. This is the reason we fight so hard to save intact families!

It is natural to be loyal to blood; but children and hurts from a previous relationship can hinder you from joining and fully weaving together.

Study a blended family for a minute and you can see just how easy it is to get triangulated between all the parties involved. If you're in a blended family, and chances are that you are in some way (if not directly, then indirectly), you know how challenging it can be to fully join with your mate. The reasons for the challenges are almost countless, and sadly, the effects are often tragic for blended families. Quite simply, and this may seem harsh, if you put any person between you and your spouse, you cannot truly join. And, yes, this even means your children.

Second marriages present a unique set of challenges. Guilt, fear, shame, frustration, and more may lead parents and family members to overcompensate and feel that their own biological child is not being treated fairly compared to attention spent on the stepchildren. Likewise, your new spouse may feel that your biological child is shown more love and respect than they are. The stories we've heard are countless, but the impact and damages are all the same. If not addressed over time, the majority of these second marriages fail. And it's not because they don't love each other. It's because they never knew or understood the need for joining.

Hold up, before you start thinking that we're advocating for dismissing children, or worse, suggesting that you neglect their needs, please hear us out! Rest assured; we absolutely are not. What we're saying is that your loyalty to your partner needs to be first—whether you're in a blended family or not. Joining and operating as a unified front is critical. The moment one of you places one or more children (even adult ones) between the two of you, or the moment things are even perceived that way, you're going down a path of trouble.

Blended families present a unique set of challenges in addition to the typical ones that families already have to deal with. Couples in a blended family need to work together to combat interference, manipulation, and the intentions of well-meaning (and not so well-meaning) others. And, at times, this will mean that choices must be made for the sake of the family and not any one individual.

It is easy to believe that no one will ever love or understand your kids as much as you do. Thus, regardless of the best intentions in blended families, there's always going to be an undercurrent of misplaced loyalties or concerns about fairness at some level. And the mixed loyalties can extend to favoritism and unfair treatment (whether perceived or real) from extended family members like grandparents or the ex. You would be the rare exception (and we would applaud you) if you're in a blended family and don't have to deal with these issues.

Therefore, seeking professional help and support for your family can save you years of heartache and possibly even stave off a divorce. Don't stuff your feelings or think they'll go away on their own. They generally intensify, not lessen, if left unaddressed.

Likewise, you also need to see that your partner may not perceive their children from a former marriage or their parents the same way you do. They may have some misplaced loyalties that blind them from seeing what you see. In this case, a soft startup and loving approach will often get more done than run-of-the-mill complaints. It's also critical to avoid using absolute statements—the "you always" and "you never" statements that only serve to bring about resistance and create a widening gap between the two of you.

The Bottom Line

Joining is a necessary element in healthy and thriving relationships. When we marry, two become one. Two individuals come together to make one marriage and that marriage is to be prioritized and protected. Cling to your mate by becoming one cohesive unit. This requires us to place our mates at a higher level of importance than anyone else in our lives—including our friends, family, and yes, even our children.

A LOOK IN THE MIRROR

1. Do you feel joined to your mate?

2. Have you ever chosen your parent or a friend over your mate? How did it make your mate feel?

3. Do you find it difficult to prioritize your mate over your child(ren)?

4. How can you show your child(ren) that you are loyal to your mate above all others?

5. Are there any hurts from your past that you need to address to better join with your mate?

6. In what way(s) do you feel disjoined from your mate?

7. If you have a blended family, in what way(s) do you feel disloyalties? Have you shared this with your mate? What was their reaction?

KNOWLEDGE

An awareness or familiarity of yourself and
your mate gained by experience.

YOU ARE INCREDIBLY SPECIAL. NOW, BEFORE YOU ROLL YOUR EYES AT us like we're some kind of motivational poster in a school hallway, hear us out. We once read a statistic that said the chances of your being born just as you are—with your eyes, your nose, your kind of hair, your height, etc.—is 1 in 400 trillion. Don't just keep reading past that. Pause. Take it in. Say it out loud. 1 in 400 TRILLION!!!!!!!!!!!! One trillion is a 1 with 12 zeros after it and we're talking 400 of those! The chances of you turning out like you is 1 in 400,000,000,000,000!!!! WOWZA!!!!!

You are more than just unique—you are a mathematical miracle! So, being different from other people (including your mate) isn't wrong; it's beautifully miraculous. You and your mate share the opportunity of not only getting to know you and what makes you so special, but also getting to know your mate and what makes him/her so special.

Knowledge is learning all the ins and outs and nitty-gritties about yourself and your mate. It includes learning from experiences with your mate, listening to your mate, asking yourself tough and reflective questions, and sometimes looking at measurable things like personality tests and assessments. There are limits to the value of such tests, but nonetheless, we consider them very valuable when used correctly.

Let's explore some of the common ways we might be different from our mates and how we can use our knowledge of these differences to enhance communication and minimize marital problems. The goal of gaining more knowledge is not to make you superior to your mate or better able to control him or her! Instead, it is to know how to enhance your awareness, minimize conflict, to avoid taking things personally, and to continue to learn and grow in your relationship.

Get to Know Your Love Languages

Most people are familiar with the Five Love Languages. If you aren't, here's a quick rundown. The Five Love Languages, developed by pastor and counselor Dr. Gary Chapman, are five different ways people generally show and receive love. Most people relate to some combination of these. They are (in no particular order): 1) quality time, 2) acts of service, 3) gifts, 4) physical touch, and 5) words of affirmation.

Do a search for the Five Love Languages and you'll find a short quiz you can take to find out which is your dominant love language. Have your mate do the same. You may learn that the way you show love may not match up with the way your mate wants it to be shown. Remember, communication of love has two pieces: delivery and acceptance. You can give an eloquent speech to your mate in Russian, but they're not going to understand it if they speak Portuguese.

Get to Know Your Personality Profile

There are a few different types of personality profile assessments out there. Two of the most popular are the 16 Myers-Briggs Personalities and the 9 Enneagrams. Both assessments take a look at varying aspects of your personality and put together some combination of preferences or tendencies.

These personality types have certain tendencies in relationships, friendships, and in the workplace. Knowing your personality type and your mate's personality type can help you spot those tendencies, better understand one another's preferences and views, and help you prepare for areas of conflict, weakness, or trouble.

Think of it this way. If you know who you are and who your mate is, you can better find ways to empathize with one another and navigate around (and sometimes through) obstacles.

Get to Know Your Thinking Style

As you're hopefully picking up on already, we all process information in different ways. And most people tend to be either 1) global thinkers or 2) linear thinkers.

Global thinkers need the big picture first and don't always go in a step-by-step order. They can be overwhelmed by the details or too many details at once. Typically, they put things together in novel or unique ways. They need the big picture in order to have the pieces fall into place. They may want to do steps out of order compared to the norm or even blend the steps together. They might ask, "Why this step?"

On the contrary, linear (or sequential) folks like details and the step-by-step approaches, processes, and procedures. They find comfort in the order and can usually see all the parts.

It is helpful to know if your mate is more of a linear or big picture person. For example, whether planning a trip around the world or around the corner to the grocery store, the global people and the linear people will approach the trip in entirely different ways. For example, the linear person might have a list organized by store aisle and go row by row. The global person might have a general idea of what they want to make for dinner and seemingly wander through the store, in what looks like a haphazard way.

Get to Know Your Primary Modes of Perception

The five basic senses are sight, sound, touch, taste, and smell. We perceive from and share information with the world through these basic senses—primarily visually, auditorily, and kinesthetically. We use and favor one sense more than others. What is your dominant or primary mode of perception?

You can use cues like word choices, posture, eye movements, and personal sensitivities to learn whether you and/or your mate are more visual, auditory, or kinesthetic.

Your mate may have different sensitivities than you. It doesn't make them irrational or difficult—it just makes them different. So, be compassionate to their preferences. While I (Kimberly) am a big fan of eye contact, I understand that a mate who isn't looking at me throughout a conversation may have his ear turned to me to better hear me—not because he isn't paying attention.

When having important conversations, listen for your mate to express themselves in their own way—what they see, hear, or feel. Try to help one another better communicate by trying your hand at using their mode of expression. If you're a visual person and your mate is auditory, for example, try saying, "I'm hearing you say …" instead of saying, "I see." Compassion is called for here because you can't experience exactly what another person is experiencing. Each individual processes in their own way.

Get to Know Your Work Style

Do you tend to be more reflective or active? What about your mate?

Reflective people prefer to work alone rather than in partnership. Active people prefer to work in groups as opposed to alone. How will you and your mate tackle tasks if one of you is reflective and one is active? Plan projects that allow you to work together for the active mate but with opportunities for the reflective person to work alone at times.

The reflective mate will need to think things out before acting and the active mate will use phrases like, "Let's try it out". Planning can be a challenge if you have two different styles. Knowing this ahead of time helps you understand and respect one another's approaches as different rather than inferior.

The reflective mate needs time alone to rest, relax, and think. If the active mate creates some "alone time" for the reflective one, they'll be deeply appreciated. For example, draw a bath for your reflective mate, and take the kids to the store or the zoo so s/he can relax! On the flip side, the active mate wants to be just that—active. If you're reflective, plan some activities together that fill their need for action or give them an opportunity for a "friends' night out".

Find Out if You're Sensing or Intuitive

We talked about perceptions, whether visual, auditory, or tactile. People also have tendencies toward being more "sensing" or more "intuitive". Like all the other dichotomies in style, each person can have a little of both.

Sensing mates prefer a hands-on approach while the intuitive mate is comfortable with the abstract. One prefers solving problems with tested and proven methods while the other has a more innovative approach to problem solving. If you and your mate have different approaches, communication and compassion will be key in handling the problems that every marriage will face with work, schedules, kids, family, house maintenance, and more.

The sensing types do not usually like surprises, while the intuitive one enjoys open possibilities. If the sensing mate surprises the intuitive one with a trip, it might be a joy. But if the intuitive mate keeps trying to surprise the sensing one, it might create discord. The sensing mate needs structure, facts, and details, while the intuitive mate abhors routine and repetition.

The sensing mate has to give the intuitive mate room to spread their adventurous wings and fly, and the intuitive mate will need to help the sensing mate with a sense of safety and security. Family ceremonies can go a long way to create a sense of stability. Planning free nights and understanding the need for spontaneity can help the intuitive mate feel alive. Couples can arrange life to meet the needs of both. The sensing mate can balance the checkbook and plan the meals for most days of the week, while one night a week will be a surprise meal to add the serendipity enjoyed by intuitive types.

Get to Know Your Response Modes

When faced with any tasks—whether it be small or large, mundane, or life-changing—we can respond with action (physically), thoughts (mentally), or feelings (emotionally). Though it may not seem so, we do not respond with these all at once. Each individual has their own order (or hierarchy) of response. It's important to know what yours is. It's also good to know if you or your mate tend to get stuck in one of these response modes.

We have an example we often use with clients to help them determine their primary response mode. Play along to help determine yours. Try the same example with your mate to find out theirs. Ready? Here we go:

Imagine that you've been experiencing some health problems, and your doctor ordered a battery of tests. Then, they call you in for an appointment. If it was good news, you think, they would have told you over the phone, so we're assuming that the news is not good.

You're now sitting in the doctor's office, and they tell you, "I'm sorry to tell you this, but you have a serious illness."

What is your immediate reaction, your knee-jerk response? Is it to demand more tests and a second opinion? To jump up from your seat and pace around the office? This would be taking action, a physical response.

Would you be overwhelmed with emotions and begin to cry? Or instantly feel scared or sad? This would be an emotional or feeling response.

Would you go into thinking mode and start processing a myriad of thoughts? For example, "The doctor said, 'serious' but didn't say 'terminal' or 'cancer'. So how bad can it be, really?" That's an analytical or thinking response.

Knowing each mate's most likely initial response is useful when processing conflict or good news. You can't be mad at your mate for not jumping for joy or getting excited if they respond to good news with mental processing. We're all different, and that's okay. (We feel like we've said this 100 times in this chapter so far, but we cannot express it enough.)

It's also valuable to look at your own hierarchy of responses. If you feel first, then act, then think, you might find yourself not thinking things through thoroughly. You might be making decisions based on emotions without adding in logic. Or, if you think first and then act, you might come off as callous because feelings don't seem to be taken into account. Ideally, we would run through all three responses and maybe even loop through them again a time or two.

Get To Know Your Basic Roles & Needs in Life

It's valuable to look at your mate's personality and understand the basic role they play naturally in life. Our research suggests that there are seven basic life roles. Other assessments might organize these differently, but ours are: Leader, Doer, Educator, Inspirer, Learner, Explorer, and Supporter. Abilities and goals may overlap some of these roles and cause them to look similar, but the basic underlying goals are different with each role.

We teach our clients the idea of having five basic needs: Adventure, Autonomy, Belonging, Certainty, and Influence. They're similar to those taught by Anthony Robbins, but he adds a sixth. Not to be confused with Maslow's hierarchy of needs, these five basic needs help you and your mate determine not only what you need to be happy and fulfilled in your life, but also your strengths and limitations. No one model is the end-all be-all, but we find this knowledge helpful in meeting one another's needs.

When you know what role you and your mate each tend to fall into and what basic needs you and your mate have most often, you can better love one another, better communicate with one another, and better find a deeper understanding of one another's motives and goals.

The Dark Side of Knowledge—A Cautionary Tale

A little bit of knowledge used the wrong way is not a good thing. Using knowledge against your mate is destructive and manipulative. For example, if you know your mate is more visual and sensitive to visual clutter, and you leave clutter in a passive aggressive way because you're upset with them, that's abusing the power of knowledge.

We had a client that threatened divorce because her mate was not using her love language.

This is the dark side of knowledge—using it to demand that they meet your needs. "You know that I'm auditory, so why would you make all that noise?"

Avoid using results from any online personality assessment or your perceived knowledge of your mate to label your mate as narcissistic, bi-polar, having a borderline personality disorder, or any of the number of mood or personality disorders. Claiming a mate is a narcissist requires a diagnosis. It is reckless for you, your mate, or a therapist to diagnose or create a treatment plan for someone that they have not properly assessed.

We have had clients come in that have personally diagnosed their mates but have never really considered that there might be other non-DSM-5 (Diagnostic and Statistical Manual of Mental Disorders, Fifth Edition) reasons for their mate's behavior.

The Bottom Line

We create a reaction with each word, choice, and interaction.

Are you considering what comes naturally to your mate and how they are uniquely different? Knowledge is power, and how you use the power is up to you. Knowledge and power can be used to build up or destroy. It is up to you. Knowledge is a tool, and like any tool, it can be used well, used poorly, or not at all. Our hope is that as you learn new information, you use it well.

> Knowledge is a tool, and like any tool, it can be used well, used poorly, or not at all.

In the absence of knowledge, we revert to assuming that our mate is just the same as we are. Or we assume that we know what they're thinking, feeling, and believing and (more importantly) why.

Ideally, we should be in an ongoing search to figure out what is happening and why. In **A is for Awareness**, we learned how to be aware of the sensitivities and things that impact our self-awareness and awareness of our mates. We also learned about the chronic and acute topics that require our awareness. It is helpful to blend awareness, knowledge, and understanding to get a fuller picture of how all these work in unison.

For more about these personality types and ways to get to know yourself and your mate, go to https://www.wordstolovebybook.com, where you will find handouts and other great resources that we normally reserve for our clients. Yes, we want to share all the goodies with you!

A LOOK IN THE MIRROR

1. What is your love language, and could you identify your mate's? How do you adapt to your mate's love language?

2. What dominant personality traits do you have? What about your mate?

3. What is your primary mode of response? And your mate's?

4. Do you know which of the seven roles in life you most align with? Which is your mate's?

5. Can you identify your mate's primary need? And yours?

6. How do you use what you know about your mate's personality and processes to better navigate difficult conversations or situations?

7. Have you ever used something you know about your mate's preferences to manipulate a situation?

LOYALTY

—

A strong feeling of support, devotion, or allegiance.

W E RECENTLY WENT TO A MILITARY CEMETERY TO PAY OUR RE-
spects to Kimberly's stepfather and mother who are both buried
there. During this visit we observed the way others paid their respects to
the veterans buried there. If you've been to a military cemetery, you can't
help but notice the unspoken bond and loyalty between military veterans and their families. Likewise, military personnel have a special bond,
regardless of the branch they served in or when they served. They seem
to always have each other's back. They are the epitome of loyal and they
can be counted on protect each other.

The dictionary may assign a definition to loyalty as being a strong
feeling of support, faithfulness, devotion, or allegiance. But what that
definition doesn't tell us is that loyalty in relationships—like the hus-
band-and-wife relationship—is actually much more than a feeling. It
is also our thoughts and in fact, loyalty requires action. It is the way we
speak to and about our partner. It is being steadfast when facing temptation. Loyalty is even found in the ways that we refuse to speak to and
about our partner.

So Much More Than Fidelity

In romantic relationships, people often jump to the idea of fidelity to
describe loyalty. Yes, fidelity in a relationship is huge, but it is only the tip
of the iceberg called loyalty. Just as most icebergs carry (hide) their mass

under the seas where you don't see it, there is far more to loyalty than one can see. We actually see fidelity as less about loyalty to your mate and more about being faithful to your vows.

We once heard someone describe loyalty as each person in the relationship holding and protecting a piece of the other person and how each person guards their piece against harm. We like that. The imagery of guarding and protecting your mate gives you purpose. It makes you feel needed and impacts the way you think about your mate.

> Loyalty is born of trust and commitment. It is not a luxury. It is not conditional.

Loyalty isn't always easy. Especially when times are challenging. It takes effort, awareness, commitment, self-sacrifice at times, and an understanding that the piece of your partner that you hold is precious and worth guarding against all forms of harm—just as your partner should hold dear the piece of you that they have been entrusted with.

Loyalty is born of trust and commitment. It is not a luxury. It is not conditional. Nor is it based on the "what have you done for me lately?" philosophy. *That is not true loyalty.* Authentic and true loyalty offers your partner security. And fosters deeper and mutual loyalty.

Loyalty is choosing your partner, even during the times when they make it hard to choose them or during times when it would be easier not to consider them. For example, if you had a big argument with your mate and you were upset with them, loyalty is resisting the temptation to flirt with someone else... or worse. Loyalty to your mate is not spending that money that you both had agreed to save, rather than blow it out of frustration, bitterness, contempt, anger, or selfishness.

Be Your Mate's Fireproof Safe

We have a fireproof safe in the house to protect our valuables. We like to think of loyalty as being a safe for our mate's vulnerabilities. What usually springs to mind when considering loyalty is faithfulness and fidelity, understandably. But loyalty in a relationship includes honesty in all other forms as well. It is being honest about your hopes, dreams, wants, desires, fears, and concerns. It is also following through. It is protecting your mate's public image. And it's keeping private things private. It's being a well-armored safe for your mate's vulnerabilities and feelings. Confidentiality is a significant part of loyalty.

Carlos felt betrayed when Susan told her friends that he lost his job. He was embarrassed because he wasn't ready to talk about it with other people yet. He felt an immense amount of pressure and saw himself as a failure. Susan's disclosure to her friends made Carlos' perceived failure feel all the more real. Susan, who was also afraid of the loss of income, chose to confide in friends rather than in Carlos. Knowing that he felt bad, she chose to take care of her own emotional needs by disclosing the information to her friends. This may be understandable, but it undermined the relationship.

Jess was upset that her partner, Todd, had "shut down" and didn't seem to be as close lately. What Jess failed to understand was the depths of violation that Todd felt when she told her best friend that Todd had been having ED problems. Todd felt that she was betraying something very private and personal from their bedroom.

Jerry openly teased his wife, Lynn, about her driving because she backed into a post in a parking lot once. Lynn identified this as being disloyal and believed that it drove a wedge between Jerry and her. If this had been a private joke between them—one that they only shared at home— she might not have felt so strongly betrayed. But every time he said something in public, she felt like he was parading her misstep for all to see. She even noticed that she had begun to limit conversations or situations that might lead to this topic coming up. In counseling, she said that if he was willing to do this, knowing that it caused her so much discomfort, she wondered what else he would say and share with his friends about her.

More Support Than Memory Foam

Being supportive and being your mate's biggest yea-sayer is a part of loyalty, too (more of that in **Y is for Yea-sayer**). Successful couples do not speak ill of their mates to others. They do not join in when someone publicly criticizes their mates. Complaining about their mates to friends or family or sharing their bad habits or missteps with the world is something that successful couples avoid. Instead, they habitually shine a positive spotlight on their mates. It's not out of fear or ignorance, but rather, out of love, respect, gratitude, and a desire to protect or shelter their partners from harm, embarrassment, or critique.

Do you stick up for your partner, even when it would be easier not to? Do you protect and guard your partner's weaknesses? What are their fears and concerns? If you need to vent about your partner, resist the urge to vent to friends, family, and co-workers. Instead, find a good therapist and vent in the sanctity of that relationship.

This may be counterintuitive, but even speaking out of turn and sharing good news (like a pregnancy, a new home, an award, or promotion) can seem disloyal to some, while it would make others feel good—like you're bragging on them. It's important to know where your mate stands on sharing information like this to avoid a feeling of disloyalty.

Loyal couples include each other in life decisions out of loyalty to their marriages and know that life decisions impact their partners and their marriages. Similarly, loyalty is also found in the commitments we make to our partners and our habits of either keeping or breaking promises and commitments. Further, loyalty is found in the way that we encourage and support our partners.

As I (Kimberly) have gotten older, I have noticed a decline in my night vision. Not dramatically so, but enough that I opt out of driving at night if I have a choice. A few months back, a girlfriend with a young child at home needed supplies while her husband was traveling for work. I was torn because I wanted to help her, but I also prefer to be cautious and not drive at night. Knowing this, Joel volunteered, without hesitation, to drive me to help her. He didn't even give it a thought. He claims that he offered because I would need help carrying things, but it was a show of loyalty to my desire to be a good friend and a way to protect me from the stress of night driving on a stormy night.

Careful Where Loyalty Lies

Loyalty, like trust, is earned. And both trust and loyalty are hard, but not impossible, to recover if lost. Trust is more of a belief or feeling, while loyalty involves actions (or, in some cases, inactions) that might violate trust or weaken loyalty. Understandably, in relationships, it is normal to experience differences in priorities. The actual differences are of less concern than how you work through the differences that strengthen or undermine loyalty.

It is not uncommon for people to experience mixed or clashing loyalties because they have loyalty to family that they've known all their lives; loyalty to a friend who has been there for them; loyalty to a coworker, a child, or a spouse. What happens when being loyal to one of these groups causes you to be disloyal (real or perceived) to another group (your mate, your family)? Honestly, it is a conflict of interest to try to be loyal to everyone. But, again, it is how you work through the challenge that results in a reinforced or weakened relationship.

I (Joel) have a realtor friend who told me that in his job, they describe loyalty as putting their client's best interest above all others. When his buyers sign a contract with him, he is legally bound to a loyalty that requires him to care more about his client's well-being than his commission, other realtors, or the sellers. While he is still bound to honesty, fairness, and ethical behavior to all parties involved, he invested in and seeks to protect his clients most. We should treat our mates as such. Our loyalty to them means we put their best interest above all others.

Doormats Wear Out Quickly

There are times when some people confuse loyalty with being manipulated, abused, or treated like doormats. Being loyal to your mate shouldn't result in your mental, emotional, or physical harm. Loyalty should be mutual, keeping vulnerabilities private. Loyalty is not an invitation for anyone to behave poorly or mistreat us.

It is not disloyal to seek professional or even legal help when your mate is abusive or acting unethically, immorally, or illegally. It is actually more of an act of loyalty to your mate to help them not harm themselves or others. Loyalty to our mates means that we protect them from areas that can cause long-term or irreparable damage to them, you, and your marriage.

The Bottom Line

We love the quote by Paulo Coelho that says, "Where there is loyalty, weapons are of no use." When we are loyal to our mates, we do not bring them harm—neither directly from us nor indirectly from our words or actions.

Loyalty isn't just protecting the marital bed. It's taking actions (or inactions) to protect your mate's privacy, weaknesses, and vulnerability. It's supporting their hopes and dreams, and it's having a mindset of putting their best interests first. With true loyalty, no weapon can harm them.

A LOOK IN THE MIRROR

1. Describe a time that you experienced disloyalty. Why do you consider it an act of disloyalty? How did you resolve the issue?

2. How do you protect your mate's public image?

3. What does being disloyal look like to you?

4. Are you a good secret keeper? Why or why not?

5. What people do you know that are good examples of loyalty?

6. Would you consider yourself a loyal mate? What about your spouse?

7. What is one way you can be more loyal to your mate and marriage?

MENDING

To repair something that is broken or
damaged; to return to health; to heal.

I (KIMBERLY) HAVE A SMALL SCAR ON MY KNEE. IT'S FAINT AND YOU probably can't see it unless I point it out to you. I got it from falling off my bike as a kid. My mom put some Neosporin on it, gave me a Band-Aid, and kissed the boo-boo. No big deal. Doesn't hurt.

I have another scar on my abdomen. This one is more prominent (and the likelihood of me showing it to anyone is 0%). This one is from a surgery I had to remove my gallbladder. That annoying organ had to go. The doctors operated, stitched me up, and told me to rest and to heal. And I did—with a few dietary changes. But there's that scar—the reminder that something in me wasn't working right and my body (and health) needed to be repaired.

> Choosing to recover from problems in a productive way is choosing to heal, to mend, and to have a healthier, happier marriage.

We've read many stories and talked to several friends who have had surgeries or injuries that resulted in some scar tissue. On the outside, it seemed that the body was healing, but meanwhile, on the inside, scar tissue was adhering to healthy tissues and organs around the wounds. Scar tissue can be painful, limit movement, or cause numbness.

With any injury or surgery, doctors give advice on how to best prevent scarring and scar tissue. Why? Because it's easier to prevent it than to treat it later. Taking preventive measures helps limit the impact of the wound.

Conflict Is Normal, Mending Is Not

Troubles, disagreements, arguments, and disappointments—metaphoric wounds—are a natural part of any relationship. If a couple says they never disagree, we are greatly concerned with what's going on! Not only is conflict natural, but—hear us out—it can be a good thing. You see, it is the mending and recovering from conflict that is the predictor of the success of a relationship. **(See C is for Conflict)**

Consider these questions that we might ask if you were a client of ours.

- When's the last time you and your mate had a disagreement?
- How did you handle it?
- What did "making up" look like?
- And who initiated it?
- Better yet, who apologized first? And how?

Choosing to recover from problems in a productive way is choosing to heal, to mend, and to have a healthier, happier marriage. The way you come back together as a couple and "stitch up the wound" determines how visible the scar is and whether you'll leave behind scar tissue.

Extending An Olive Branch

Whatever the disagreement or trouble is over, Reach Outs and Olive Branches (ROOBs) are necessary for healing from it.

Historically, the olive branch has symbolized peace. In Ancient Rome and Greece, olive branches were given after Olympic Games to the victors, and they were also often worn in weddings by brides. In the Christian faith, we see artwork depicting a dove (representing the Holy Spirit) carrying an olive branch in its mouth (symbolic of bringing peace). In the story of Noah and the flood, Noah sends out a dove to check to see if the flood waters have receded. The dove returns carrying an olive branch in its mouth—showing that the flood had dried enough to rebuild. Pictures of olive branches have even made their way onto peace treaties and other agreements between nations.

What tangible things do you do to extend an olive branch to your mate when there is or have been problems? Your peace offering might be making your mate a cup of coffee just the way they like it. Or maybe you've heard the stereotypical story of a man bringing home flowers when he is in the "doghouse". One client of mine lives to do Sudoku puzzles and has shared how her husband buys her Sudoku books after disagreements to extend an olive branch. Some people show their love and effort to make up by gifting their mates a small token of affection— her favorite candy bar, his favorite food, a sentimental greeting card, etc.

"Reach outs" are like olive branches but instead of a tangible token of affection, it's more of a gesture, word, or action. These may be a kiss, a touch, or simply saying, "I'm sorry," or "I love you". Maybe he does the dishes or cooks supper for you. Perhaps she scratches your back. Reach outs are more like an act of service to your mate or a kind word of encouragement, appreciation, remorse, or affirmation.

John Gottman, a well-known marriage and relationship researcher, calls these actions "Bids for Connection". A *bid* is an attempt made by one mate to the other for attention, affirmation, affection, or some other form of positive *connection*. This could be something as simple as a wink or a smile or perhaps asking your mate for help or advice.

Whatever you call them—reach outs, olive branches, bids for connections or something else entirely—wildly successful marriages are made of two people who are willing to do them and *accept* them. Check that italicized word again—*accept* them. We have to recognize when our partners are extending the olive branch and trying to mend—and when they aren't quite ready to.

Terri Clarke, a country singer, has a song called *I Just Wanna Be Mad (For a While)*. You gotta love the honesty of the song. Her lyrics basically say that she is not leaving her man, but she isn't ready to make up with him just yet. Ladies, this may be surprising, but one of your man's greatest fears is that you will leave him. That is a legit concern since the primary filers of divorce are women. Extending an olive branch or bid for connection can signal to your man that everything is going to be okay—eventually. It doesn't have to mean that you're back to normal or ready to jump into his arms, but it can signal that you're committed to healing and mending.

I Accept Your apology

The most successful couples learn, understand, and recognize what actions and behaviors their partners use when they are attempting to mend. These couples also make a habit of not snapping the olive branch off when it is extended. They offer apologies and they accept them when offered.

Do you know your mending style? What reach outs or olive branches work for you? And what do you do that tells your partner you're mending?

People learn much of how to mend from their upbringing. Do you offer ROOBs the way you saw your mom or dad offer it? If it works, great! But don't be afraid to try something different if it's not as effective as you would like. You can change and make course corrections to refine your mending style. Communicating about mending with your partner is important. You may even want to discuss with your parents whether their mending style worked for them or not.

Something that is a challenge for me (Kimberly) is that I used to find it hard to get un-upset (we think we just made up a word). I admit I am capable of stewing on things and finding it hard to let them go. Now, to combat this, if I am upset about something, I give myself a time limit. I tell myself that I can be upset until, say, Tuesday at 5, then I need to move on or talk about it. It gives me time to sit with whatever is bothering me so I can filter emotions and get to the core of what is truly upsetting me.

It allows me time to plan for getting un-upset. But it also says that I can't stay there forever. No grudge holding here.

The Positive-to-Negative Ratio

Relationship researcher John Gottman insists that your marriage needs five positive interactions for every one negative interaction—otherwise, the negative interactions chip away at your relationship's underpinnings. Think about the positive interactions as filling the love tank of your relationship so the negative ones don't drain it or cause it to run on fumes. Just as a car depleted of gas and oil will face costly internal damages, so will a marriage running on too many negatives and not enough positives.

Although this relationship book contains all the elements of creating and sustaining a successful marriage, we will be the first to tell you that there is no precise formula for love and successful marriages. One thing is absolutely necessary: You have to have more positive interactions than negative ones (understandably).

Gottman's 5-to-1 ratio is actually quite simplistic. Not all "interactions" are considered equal. You know that not all offenses cause the same damage and not all positive interactions build the same intimacy. The ratio that fills the needs of your marriage has to account for both of you as individuals, including your past experiences. Some couples need an 8-to-1 ratio; for others, a 4-to-1 ratio might be fine for the stage they're in. We've found that the ratio is less important than how the couple interacts and treats each other in general. This applies even more to the day-to-day activities and general disposition of each spouse. Are you warm to each other, or abrupt and callous? Does your mate's behavior tell you that you matter to them, and they care for you?

The positive-to-negative ratio reminds us to make intentional efforts at positive interactions. Just as physical scars can be minimized with Vitamin E and cocoa butter, so can the scars of relationship wounds.

Cushion your hearts with random acts of kindness, supportive and appreciative words, and genuine affection. Then, when you hit a bump or take a fall, the damage won't be nearly as bad. That negative experience doesn't do the same damage when you've had lots of positive interactions to build a solid foundation of love.

Grudge Holders Beware

There is a quote circulating on social media that says something like, "Happy marriages are made up of two good forgivers." We like that. We've never met a grudge holder who seemed very happy.

People withhold forgiveness for a number of reasons, and they may feel quite justified in those reasons. Perhaps they think they should not have to forgive or that they should get to be right. Maybe they're afraid to forgive because they think it lets the offender off the hook or that the harm they did didn't matter. Maybe they think that the other person doesn't deserve to be forgiven, or that the hurts were too deep to forgive, or that the offending spouse must be held accountable for what they did. Some people hold out on forgiveness because they think their mate should have to ask for it first, that they need more time before they can forgive, or that their mate needs to suffer a while more.

In order to forgive, we have to release the mindset of having to be right and search instead for happiness. Forgiveness is releasing someone from the debt they owe you so that YOU can move on. It avoids holding others responsible for your happiness, blaming others for how you feel, or believing that you're the victim. Forgiving them for their wrong releases the burden you carry of that grudge; it allows you to move forward from your present state.

Yes, forgiveness can be difficult. Sometimes it's really hard. And yes, it's understandable that some things are easier to forgive than others. Forgiving an affair will take a lot longer and far more effort than your mate's insensitive comments about your brother. But, if you want to eventually mend and enjoy a healthy marriage, forgiveness and managing conflict well is not optional—it's a must.

Failure to forgive leads to bitterness. And bitterness is a terrible poison that threatens even the strongest of unions. Bitterness leads to the destruction of your marriage.

The 4 Rs

Oftentimes there is a tendency to shove hurt and pain aside in an attempt to reconcile. Sweeping things under the rug is not really mending. It's diverting and circumventing the process of forgiveness by going directly to reconciliation and not forgiving. True mending requires both forgiveness and reconciliation.

While forgiveness is happening, so must reconciliation through the 4 Rs: Remorse, Responsibility, Repair, and Restitution. You do these to show (1) Remorse for the hurt you inflicted without excuses or blaming others for your actions, and (2) You take responsibility for your actions and motives and accept the consequences that arise as a result. Next, (3) you do whatever you can to repair the damage you caused. (4) Some call this step restitution. Let's add a fifth R and say that (5) it is important to make changes in your decisions and actions to prevent you from *Repeating* the hurt you caused.

Marriages can't mend if you forgive but don't reconcile. And you can't mend if you reconcile but don't truly forgive. Forgiveness and reconciliation work hand in hand and require action by both parties—forgiveness AND reconciliation.

Faux Forgiveness Isn't Real Forgiveness

Some people are quick to forgive and even take on more than their share of the blame. Others say they have forgiven, only to bring up the offense again and again. We see this as faux forgiveness (faux meaning fake), and we see it often. After all, if you say you've forgiven but keep bringing up the offense over and over again, have you really forgiven?

Johnston and Julia are dealing with faux forgiveness. Over a year ago, Johnston disclosed that he had an affair, and Julia was rightly, deeply hurt. They came in for help to save the marriage. He admitted fault and acknowledged the damage to the marriage. Julia, however, insisted that she had forgiven him and desperately wanted to repair the marriage and make it work. Yet, each session, she found a way to jab, criticize, or remind him of his indiscretion. It was so blatant that it was clear: all she wanted to do was beat him up. Worse yet, she wanted us to join her in flogging her husband! Further, she resisted looking deeper at what the affair said to and about her and why she felt such a need to verbally assault and ridicule him.

Now, before you conclude that we've sided with Johnston, you should understand that if our clients say they want to save their marriage, we side with what is best for creating a strong, healthy marriage—not him, not her. Marriages that are weathering some sort of indiscretion or deep wound need to get into a positive climb rate. They need to get past and above the turbulence if they want to be stronger on the other side.

Another client, Tanya, was also dealing with an indiscretion in her marriage. The break in trust shook her to the core, but just like Julia, Tanya resisted forgiveness and healing and kept venting about her husband's indiscretion. She said that she needed to get the poison out. But each week after sessions, she would go home and listen to her girlfriends tell her that she needed to make him pay and not forgive him. Her friends are not living her life and were not helping her mend. They kept pulling the scab off and poking the wound, making it impossible for her to heal and forgive.

For both Tanya and Julia, it is not enough to say they forgive their husbands. Their actions must show it also if they intend to mend. Continuing to fuss at our mates or vent with our friends is not taking the necessary actions associated with forgiveness.

On the other side of the coin is Sheree, whose mate had an affair, and she took on all the responsibility for his indiscretion. She decided that it was her fault and absolved him of blame. This is unbalanced and an unstable relationship. Sheree's husband, Doug, is letting her take the blame so he can feel off the hook. And some partners will manipulate situations for just that reason—so their partners take on all or more than their share of the blame. It's important not to take all the responsibility for a co-created situation.

These situations are great examples of why it's so important to learn how to do conflict effectively. Every relationship has conflict. (Review **C is for Conflict**.) Learning how to navigate it so that it grows into a stronger relationship is the goal. The process of forgiveness is to understand the story of the story, and that, too, is part of mending.

The Ancient Art of Mending

The Japanese art of Kintsugi is the art of mending broken pottery into something more beautiful, powerful, and stronger than ever. It takes broken chunks of pottery and mends them together with gold. When you look at a piece of Kintsugi art, you don't see the brokenness or shards of clay that could have been tossed in the trash. Instead, you see flowing veins of gold giving the pottery new character, new meaning, new value, and new life.

Our marriages could use some Kintsugi work. When we offer our mates our brokenness and our hurts and we work to mend our problems and troubles, we rebuild and redefine our relationship. We mend pieces back together with gold and solidarity. We create something even more beautiful than before—something that could not have been if we had not once chipped some edges or broken some pieces.

The Bottom Line

Marriage, like all things in life, can be tough at times. Disagreements are natural and how we deal with them can determine the health of our relationship. Seeking peace after an argument can begin by extending an olive branch to your mate—maybe by giving them a kiss or an apology. Furthermore, healing progresses when the olive branch is received instead of rejected.

Mending from hurt requires us to forgive and seek reconciliation. Like the Kintsugi art, sometimes our biggest cracks and breaks bring about the greatest beauty. Our marital troubles don't have to leave us broken, but instead can create an opportunity for beautifully nursing our marriages into even greater health than before.

Mending is based on awareness and attunement. It's living intentionally and desiring to grow. It takes hope and engagement and is the act of resolving and moving forward with new understanding. Mending is not just *getting past* an issue but *growing past* an issue.

A LOOK IN THE MIRROR

1. What type(s) of olive branches do you extend to your mate when mending?

2. What type(s) of olive branches does your mate extend to you when mending?

3. How long does it usually take for you and your mate to make up?

4. Today, log your interactions with your mate in a journal. How many are positive, and how many are negative?

5. Is forgiving your mate harder or easier for you than forgiving other people?

6. What actions (beyond an apology) do you and your mate take to mend?

7. Looking back over your marriage, can you identify a time when healing from a hurt or a problem eventually brought about a deeper bond between you and your mate?

NOVELTY

—

The quality of being new, original, unique, or unusual.

WE'RE FASCINATED BY INFOMERCIALS. IT'S NOT THAT WE EVER BUY anything they are advertising, but we do love to watch them anyway. Odd? Probably. Ashamed? Not at all! Maybe you're curious as to why, and it's simple. We're intrigued by the novelty of the products. Many are unique and different from anything we've seen before. Yes, they're often unnecessary and some are probably even scams, but they're new and unusual, and we love to see what people will come up with next! Maybe this explains why we also like programs like *Shark Tank,* and the restaurant and bar "rescue" shows. We enjoy watching people solve problems in new and unique ways.

> A lack of novelty is one of the reasons that relationships grow stagnant and fall apart.

It is human nature to notice novelty and seek newness. Maybe it harkens back to the time when we were hunters and gatherers, always on the lookout for food and for things that might do us harm. Honestly, we humans are a restless lot. We're not at our best when stagnated. We need to be moving forward, backward, or sideways or we risk stagnation. Stagnation does not bring out our best.

Our relationships are similar. When marriages become stale and stagnant and boredom sets in, mates can stray, become apathetic, or withdraw from one another. On the contrary, couples who incorporate novelty find their lives and marriages to be more fulfilling, more loving, and more intimate.

Understanding Me-ness and We-ness

We all understand the differences between the words "me" and "we". But do we understand how me-ness and we-ness play out in creating wildly successful marriages?

Me-ness and we-ness can be envisioned by imagining each spouse as a circle. Play along and imagine that each circle is a color. We like to use yellow and blue, or pink and blue, but you can picture it whatever way you prefer.

Imagine now that these two individual circles as are 1) tangent circles barely touching, 2) almost completely overlapped circles stacked on one another, or 3) circles semi-overlapping.

For a free Me-ness-We-ness handout,
visit https://www.WordsToLoveByBook.com

Which would you think is the best representation of the strongest marriage? Barely touching, semi-overlapping, or almost overlapped? If you're like 90% of the couples we've worked with, you might say that the circles that are nearly completely overlapping best represent the goal of a successful marriage.

Let's explore these three circles and understand how novelty plays a part in which of the three truly represents the most wildly successful marriage.

Contiguous Circles (Barely Touching or Slightly Overlapping)

If the circles are barely touching or overlap only slightly, then you have two lives that are barely interacting. These individuals are essentially living separate lives and have very few shared experiences. This produces a lack of connection, intimacy, and relationship security. This is common in relationships experiencing marital troubles or in a separated couple.

The couple may have been more semi-overlapping at one time, but the circles are now moving apart. Maybe both partners are migrating away from each other, or maybe just one seems to be drifting away. Either way, their lives are less and less involved with each other, and they may be headed for a breakup.

Sometimes military spouses will identify with this image while their mate is TDY (Temporary Duty Orders). Or maybe it's a couple whose work requires long distances or times apart. In these cases, intentional effort needs to be put in for them to maintain a connection. Unfortunately, absence doesn't always make the heart grow fonder.

In the early stages of a relationship, there is so much that couples don't know about each other. They stay up late talking on the phone to learn all about the other person—knowing full well they'll have to drag themselves to work the next day and survive on coffee. They ask lots of questions, think about each other often, and have a strong desire to spend time with each other. They are curious about all the stuff in each other's circle that they don't know about yet or haven't shared. They want to close the gap between the known and the unknown. They want their individual circles to grow together. They want their colored circle to merge with the other colored circle to create something new—a new color, unique to them as a couple—like a yellow and blue merging to make one vibrant new green.

A lack of novelty is one of the reasons that relationships grow stagnant and fall apart. Couples that consistently make new memories often cite feelings of a greater connection, whether it be from watching grandchildren, frequently going on date nights, traveling, trying new activities together (even if they decide it's not for them!), or verbally sharing their individual activities with each other. It builds a shared history, and a shared history gives us the feelings of connectedness and belonging. And the novelty and unknown aspects of these activities also revive a little bit of the honeymoon phase.

Highly Overlapped (Stacked) Circles

Highly overlapping or stacked circles can be the most difficult to navigate. Seems contradictory, right? But let us explain. In the overlapping relationship, the lives of the couple are very intertwined, which seems like it should be a positive thing—even a goal. But research indicates that couples who identify with the overlapping circles will report things like feeling smothered, bored, restricted, and limited by the relationship. This is because the relationship can lack the novelty, individuality, and newness that would help keep things fresh and interesting.

The highly overlapping circles best represent a relationship where one partner of the couple is dominated and the other is domineering. The domineering partners making more of the decisions for the couple. It may even be an abusive or controlling relationship. This is not always the case, but often a concern.

The highly overlapping circles might also represent an isolated couple. These mates don't have much of a social life or friendships and relationships outside their home. For whatever reason, whether location, busy schedules, etc., these couples have become distant from other people.

While this seems counterintuitive, these couples who lack novelty need to be careful of the temptation of having affairs. These couples may complain of being "bored" and missing "excitement". They may have "shiny object" syndrome. Much like Abu, the monkey in *Aladdin* behaved, their attention may easily divert to people who seem more intriguing. Because they lack novelty in their marriage, they may seek it in someone outside of the marriage.

For couples that have been together for decades or in the later years of life, stacked circles are not uncommon. While healthy couples hope to grow closer with time, and greatly overlapping circles are very common with long term marriages, it is still important that couples have their own activities and find novelty together. It could be exploring travel together, new foods, music, or other activities. This helps empty nesters rekindle the intimacy and excitement of the honeymoon phase. It's also incredibly important with retirees who need to do things with their new-found time. Otherwise, they may feel as if they are withering away. Just be careful not to seek so much novelty that your circle grows and drifts away from your mate.

Semi-Overlapped (Linked) Circles

Two lives that are moderately overlapped or semi-overlapped have a sense of strong connection where they overlap, but enough other interests and activities in non-overlapping areas to provide novelty and autonomy. These could be things one spouse does on their own like joining a quilting circle, taking an art class, golfing with buddies, volunteering for a charity, attending a book club, learning a foreign language, enjoying a car club, or engaging with some other hobby or interest.

While we desire to be fully known and accepted, the flip side of the coin is the desire for novelty and curiosity in our lives: new experiences, new ideas, new activities, and new conversations. New experiences in the overlap areas with our mates can provide some of the need for novelty, but normally, the happiest couples have some activities apart in addition.

Ideally, the experiences and activities outside of a marriage can fulfill your need for learning, creativity, joy, and friendship that your marriage may not. Friendships and activities with others are ways to fill your cup and bring back newness and adventure into your life and relationship. It is not uncommon for bitterness to creep in when one or both partners give up a friendship or interests for the sake of the marriage. In an attempt to grow closer, we released a bit of our individual circles, but remember that the loss of novelty can be felt deeply and not always fully understood. Asking our clients if they gave up activities or interests for the relationship can be very telling. We have had clients break down crying because they gave up an interest and have never grieved or shared with their mate what that meant to them.

It is unrealistic and unfair to expect your mate to be everything to you. Even in the healthiest of relationships, you have to remember that you are two separate people with different backgrounds, interests, abilities, and even sometimes different hopes, goals, and dreams.

Some will disagree, but we hold a firm conviction that your mate should not be your "best friend". Your mate should be your lover, your most loyal and biggest supporter, your foundation, your rock, and a confidant—but not necessarily your "friend". A great mate will possess many of the same great qualities as a healthy friendship, but they are your mate. Honestly, girlfriend talk is not the same as a conversation with your mate, and neither is "guy talk". Conversations with your friends are important, even necessary. Friendship should help fill your cup and bring novelty into your circle.

In Kimberly's INLOVE program, the N stands for "nurturing your circle". It's about having novelty and experiences in your life. There is value in expanding your circle of friendships. This is one of the reasons that social media is so popular and, if used well, it can provide novelty that we need. Expecting your mate to meet all your needs is unrealistic. Furthermore, if your mate is your best friend, you are more likely to develop a stacked circle relationship.

Remember, two semi-overlapped circles nearly always produce the strongest and happiest relationships.

The Ebb & Flow of Your Circles

It needs to be noted that the three positions of circles that represent me-ness and we-ness are not static. We need to realize that relationships "breathe". At any given moment, you will be moving towards or away from your mate. The goal is to be aware of what is happening and why. Strive for the middle ground and balance and avoid too much or too little eclipsing in the relationship.

In healthy relationships, people understand the ebb and flow in a relationship. They do not panic and throw in the towel when their circles drift a bit, nor do they withdraw or attack their partner. Instead, they have a sense of relationship safety and can allow their partner breathing room, especially if their partner is dealing with something. They're also willing to engage, ask questions, and as needed, make necessary changes to themselves for the benefit of the relationship.

In a new relationship, novelty is easy. Healthy relationships include the novelty born out of newness. In long-term relationships, novelty is crucial to resolving problems. Couples can find new approaches to effectively communicate and resolve conflict. They can take approaches that their parents and others didn't try. Honestly, conflict brings novelty. Resolved conflict is a new agreement, and something new is thus novel.

Ways to Bring Novelty

We are the types of people who love learning about other cultures and traditions. It's fascinating to see how different groups of people think and act, and what they value in life. For people like us novelty comes easy, but for others the struggle can be real.

With that being said, if this chapter has you looking for ways to incorporate something new in your relationship, here's a quick list of 5 things you can do to bring back some novelty.

- *Pick a new destination.* We know some couples who vacation in the same place every year for years on end. Maybe you even have a vacation home in a favorite location. This year, pick a totally new place—somewhere you have never been as a couple. Find a place you can explore, try new restaurants, and experience new sights, sounds, and people. You may decide you love it there or you may decide to never visit there again. Either way, you've made new memories.

- *Set up monthly girls'/guys' nights out.* We know a couple who goes their own way the third Friday of every month. They get a sitter, and she goes out with her friends while he goes out with his friends. This way, neither can say they gave up their friends for the marriage, and both get the fulfillment that only their friendships can bring. It also gives them new things to share with each other about their nights out and their friends.

- *Share your hopes and dreams.* Every so often, reevaluate your hopes and dreams as individuals and as a couple. Chances are that dreams from your 20s will differ from those in your 50s. The person you got to know when you started dating has more than likely changed or evolved over the time. That's okay and natural. You both grow, learn, and change. Sharing and navigating these changes together is what keeps novelty alive instead of moving apart.

- *Have new sex.* Hopefully that didn't make you blush too much. Surprise your mate with something new tonight—a new outfit, new position, or new location for your marital bliss. As the relationship goes, so goes the sex. Looking to bring some newness to your marriage? Mix it up sexually, too ;-)

- *Pursue a new interest or hobby.* Come up with one interest that you each have. Then, either pursue it separately or together. If you pursue activities together, take a balanced approach and alternate whose interests you participate in monthly or seasonally. He may not like reading, but he can listen and learn about what she's enjoying in the latest novel in her book club. She may not like classic cars, but she can appreciate his attention to detail and be willing to attend the club's annual picnic.

The Bottom Line

Novelty is that sense of newness we get in life, not just from sharing new experiences with our mates, but also through others. It's the activities we share with friends and mates as well as the activities we participate in separately that give us new perspectives, new conversation points, new excitement, and new fulfillment in life. Novelty in our relationships keeps us from being bored and stagnant. Also, approaching conflict in novel ways helps keep our marriages strong.

Find activities you can share with your mate—travel opportunities or hobbies you participate in together. Talk about what you do and don't enjoy and look for fresh excitement. But don't trap your mate and limit them (or you) to only activities as a couple. Spread your reach and extend your novelty in your friendships. Maintain a sense of individuality with your own personal hobbies and interests. Give your mate new things to learn about you and seek to learn new things about your mate.

A LOOK IN THE MIRROR

1. Why is the newness of the dating phase so exciting?
2. Would you describe your relationship as circles barely touching, stacked, or semi-overlapping?
3. What changes would be necessary to become semi-overlapping circles if you're not already?
4. What shared activities do you and your mate participate in as a couple?
5. What hobbies or interests do you have as an individual—either with friends or alone?
6. What hobbies or interests does your mate have as an individual—apart from you?
7. What is one way you can bring novelty to your relationship at this stage in your marriage?

OPPORTUNITY

—

*Circumstances that make it possible to know,
serve, support, and grow with your mate; a
moment, time, or chance to be used wisely.*

JOEL AND I LOVE A GOOD QUOTE. SOMETIMES, TO LET OUT SOME creative energy, I'll use a graphic design program to make memes with quotes for our social media pages. You may like to paint or draw, but I doodle with graphics. We came across a quote during our research for this chapter (and who knows, maybe I'll make a graphic of it) that said, "If a window of opportunity appears, don't pull down the shade." And we kinda really loved it.

Opportunities present themselves daily. Whether it is the opportunity to encourage someone, take a risk, make a change, or serve another, opportunity is all around.

Sometimes we can even create an opportunity when it seems there isn't one. All of you go-getters who aren't fans of sitting around and waiting for an opportunity may go out there and find or make your own opportunities. Do you "pull down the shade" or do you dive right in?

> Opportunity is about looking for ways to make your marriage stronger.

Your marriage is full of opportunities, too. The happiest couples make an active habit of looking for and using opportunities to create a wildly successful marriage. They look for an opportunity to say, "I know you. I get you. I notice you. I value you. And I love you—even on the days I may not *like* you."

Opportunity is about looking for ways to make your marriage stronger. It's about seeking and *finding* an opportunity to serve, support, and grow with your partner and marriage.

Opportunities to Witness

One of the most heart-tugging movie scenes—in our very "experienced" cinematic opinion— comes from the movie *Shall We Dance?* In the movie, Susan Sarandon tells a private investigator the reason she believes people get married: "Because we need a witness to our lives. There are a billion people on the planet. I mean, what does one life really mean? But in a marriage, you are promising to care about everything—the good things, the bad things, the terrible things, the mundane things. All of it. All the time, every day. You're saying that your life will not go unnoticed, because I will notice it. Your life will not go unwitnessed, because I will be your witness."

Every single one of us wants to be known by someone. We want to be seen, understood, valued, and supported. We want someone to notice the way we laugh, appreciate our silly quirks, and be a witness to the things we work so very hard at. This is a need and a role you can play for your spouse. You get a front row seat at their life and the chance to be their #1 fan and cheerleader.

Are your eyes fixed on your mate? Do you see the things they show you each day? Are your ears open to them? Are you hearing the things they say to you and others? Be an observant witness to their life. Engage with them. Take note of their efforts and celebrate their accomplishments.

Look for an opportunity to say, "I promise to be a witness to your life and to show that you, indeed, matter." Intentionally look for opportunities and chances to connect. Always look for opportunities to validate, encourage, or come alongside your mate and tell them that they're important and valued.

I, Joel, am in a Mustang car club. It's not really Kimberly's thing, but she goes to the picnics and participates, demonstrating support for my interests and letting me know that my interests matter. In turn, I support her crafts and interests such as her letter-boarding habit (even though it borders on addiction and may require a 12-step program in the future!).

Since we're writing about opportunity, here's a personal example to share:

Kimberly: "Honey, help me remember to put the laundry in the dryer."

Joel: "Anything in there that requires special handling?"

Kimberly: "No, they're just linens."

Joel: (*Gets up and moves the clothes to the dryer and then comes back.*) "Done. Now you can go back to focusing on your writing." (*Big smile*)

Kimberly: (*Blows him a kiss.*)

Of course, not every laundry interaction has gone this well.

Joel: "Hey I got those white towels started you wanted—even remembered to add the bleach."

Kimberly: "Did you move my new blouse to the dryer?"

Joel: "New blouse, what new blouse?"

Kimberly: Sprints to the washer pulls out her new (now tie-dyed) blouse.

Joel: "Where was that?"

Kimberly: "How could you not have seen it?"

Understandably, Kimberly wasn't at all happy about it at the time. As the years have gone by, her initial ire has turned to humor as we now openly joke about it. Especially on the days she's still wears it—it's now infamously known as Kimberly's Woodstock blouse! Hey, who knew you could use a little bit of bleach and your washing machine to make tie-dyed shirts?

Opportunities to Overcome

Successful couples look for opportunities to overcome challenges—to turn difficult times into something better so they can be stronger on the other side. We talked about this in **M is for Mending**—seeking opportunities to grow the relationship, recover from struggles, and head things off at the pass.

Successful couples learn how to do conflict management. It's the cornerstone to every successful marriage. Let us let you in on a secret... Ready?... Here goes... Every relationship has conflict. Yep, they all do. That couple down the street who have the seemingly picture-perfect life—they have conflict too! But the wildly successful couples do not see conflict and disagreements as a sign to run, turn against their mate, or worst, end the relationship. Instead, they look at conflict as an opportunity to grow, evolve, and learn—not a reason to throw in the towel.

We are stressing this point because too many people think that if they have disagreements or conflicts, then that means something is wrong with the relationship or that they're not a good match. *"Maybe he wasn't Mr. Right,"* or, *"Maybe she wasn't who I was supposed to be with."* Conflict is normal, and it can be healthy when you find a way to work through it and grow from it!

However, if conflict resorts to violence, seek help immediately. And, if a nonviolent conflict is not getting resolved or is ignored, then the relationship may be in trouble, and this type of conflict is *not* healthy, good, or constructive.

Counseling can work wonders if both parties are willing to exalt the relationship over individual needs. Make sure you find a therapist that understands the difference between couples therapy and individual therapy. A highly effective couples' therapist will not side with either party. Instead, they'll treat you as a couple and set the health of the marriage as the priority. Couples' counseling is an opportunity to correct unhealthy conflict styles and learn effective ways to communicate and resolve problems.

Don't "draw the shade" on an opportunity for couples counseling. It's not an admission of problems as much as it is a statement of wanting to grow as much as you can.

Opportunities to Support

Seek out opportunities to help carry your partner's load. When your partner is stuck in the valley, our job is to throw them a pulley, ladder, and/or a climbing rope. And likewise, they should do this for you. This is an opportunity to be supportive, not an opportunity to berate and criticize your mate and their choices.

Is your mate considering a career change? How can you support a wise decision and calm their fears? Your mate may be carrying a heavy load from work, family, friends, or something else that can weigh a person down mentally and emotionally. Look for opportunities to come alongside your mate during a difficult season to support them. You may not be able to "fix" the problem (and it might be frustrating for your spouse to see that you're trying to), but you *can* carry more weight at home, with the kids, or in your marriage while your mate wades through troubled waters.

Opportunities to Serve

Find a way to serve your mate. Look for opportunities to step up and ease your partner's burden. Even if it's not YOUR thing, but it's THEIR thing, do it! Do things for the sake of the other person. Suck it up for their sake or for the bigger picture.

In many ways, it seems that people have become more selfish and will refuse to do things because it isn't "their" thing. That's the "what's in it for me?" attitude, and that type of mindset creates an unstable marital foundation, takes the focus off the marriage, and sets you up for competing with your mate. Instead, make the "what's in it for *us?*" philosophy your mantra! This leads to better communication and gives you an opportunity (there's that word again!) to put teamwork into play. Want to be successful in the long run? Place more value on your marriage than on each of you as an individual.

Interestingly, it seems that in conflict, the first thing we throw out the window is working *together*. We often use the analogy of a boat to explain the importance of this. Couples are like a boat in the water, and it doesn't always matter how the water got in the boat. However, if the boat takes on too much water, you are both going to get wet and potentially drown as the boat sinks. Borrowing from this analogy, we will ask clients if their actions are drilling holes in the shared boat or perhaps puncturing a hole in their life raft.

How is opportunity acted out? Through service and being flexible. Opportunity without service is incomplete. And service should be offered in ways that your partner desires and needs—a movie night at home after a long work week, going out to eat at a restaurant rather than dirtying up the kitchen, or taking the kids somewhere on your own so your mate can have alone time to destress and decompress.

And hear us clearly when we say that serving your partner does not mean being a doormat or being subjected to abuse or intimidation. Nor does it mean tolerating their bad or destructive behavior. For example, if your partner is entertaining unhealthy sexual interests which you find morally offensive or that triggers past or present hurts, you do not have to subject yourself to those acts out of a sense of "service". A healthy marital sexual relationship serves to better the marriage by being physically pleasurable and emotionally fulfilling for *both* mates. See **X is for X-Factor** for more on this topic.

Two people who both want a wildly successful marriage will have a desire to serve their marriage by serving their mate. In fact, healthy couples look to overserve each other and do not mind doing it because it's neither a task, nor a chore, nor a sacrifice. Rather, it's an investment in something greater than each of them as individuals.

A Word of Caution

Sadly, some (too many) people only serve their marriage when expecting a tit for tat. "I will give this, but only if he/she does that," or "I will put forth the effort, but only if they do, too." It is pretty common in counseling for couples in distress to have one or both mates say they will only put effort in "once I see them do it". Understandably, people don't want to put the effort in if it won't pay off. But one person putting in the effort can be the catalyst that changes the course of the marriage. It is often unnecessary to have both partners pulling (although that's ideal) to stimulate a course change.

Of course, there are limits. We should not be codependents or doormats, and we should avoid a relationship with a narcissist. In **S is for Safety** and **T is for Trust**, we will go into boundaries, limits, safety, narcissism, etc. Those chapters are helpful to knowing your red flags and equipping yourself to set necessary and healthy limits. You'll want to use that information to choose wise opportunities.

Some will disagree, but we have come to learn that codependency is an old and somewhat antiquated idea based on the addiction culture. The addiction model suggests that you (the codependent) are dependent on your spouse's addiction, who is not dealing with their stuff. It implies that you find a positive self-identity in helping that addictive person, with the two of you acting in concert, almost like a dance.

There are three entities in a marriage—your partner, you, and the relationship. In the traditional codependency model, the codependent individual gives up their authentic identity and in turn gets a new identity born out of their partner's dysfunction. That addicted person needs them, so they must sacrifice themselves to meet the need and be a good person.

A better term for avoiding codependency is "differentiation of self". It is learning to differentiate your own identity apart from the other person. You can be supportive but not let your identity wane or dissolve. Strong relationships are built on being wanted—not necessarily on being needed.

Bob is habitually attracted to women who "need" him. These are women, who appear to "need fixing," but Bob's relationships always seem to crash and burn. Bob is under the false notion that if they need him, he's found someone to be a loyal partner and is now secure. What Bob fails to realize is that once that need can be met by some other means (whether person or thing), his value is markedly depreciated.

Bob's habit is to focus on needs; yet healthy couples are made of two people that *want* each other, not necessarily *need* each other. If two people truly want each other, then looking for opportunities to contribute to a happier, more successful life together is natural.

Dig into yourself and ask, "Am I looking to be wanted or needed?" Be honest. Are you a conscientious giver? Do you give freely to your mate for the sole purpose of contributing to their well-being without the possibility of a return on your "investment"? Or are you scorekeeping and expecting something in return for any kindness you showed?

The happiest couples we know are the ones who look for opportunities to learn about their mates, to grow together, and to lighten their mate's burdens. If you're hopping around in the book like I, Kimberly, would be doing (there's my ADHD showing), you might have not read **K is for Knowledge** or **U is for Understanding** yet. Both of these are important elements to grasp if you want to master opportunity.

Luck Meets Preparation and Opportunity

I, Kimberly, have a memory of camping with my dad when I was a kid that has stuck with me for over 50 years. There was some sort of problem, and my dad fixed it. I said that it was lucky that he had the necessary tool, and he said, very matter-of-factly, "It isn't luck. It's preparation." I learned that day that advance planning and preparedness make all the difference between a small inconvenience and a big problem.

Roman philosopher Seneca says, "Luck is what happens when preparation meets opportunity." This is true in relationships, too. Many relationship problems are "head-off-at-the-passable". Consider these common occasions that create tensions in relationships and how advance discussion and preparation can reduce or minimize their impact.

- Christmas with the in-laws, who love to take cheap jabs or pick at your mate, leaving your mate feeling verbally battered and abused.

- Thanksgiving, when Aunt Mary drinks too much, Grandpa Ralph always tells war stories, the favorite sister gets all the accolades, the talk's all about the younger brother's achievements, and the questions are always about when you'll be having babies, etc.

- Graduations, weddings, and other events in blended families that require interaction with the other birth parent.

Each of these scenarios (and more) is a potential opportunity for conflict, which could instead be turned into an opportunity to head off conflict at the pass. Set your mate up for success in difficult situations or conversations. Consider the timing, the setting, and other things on their mind. Go into events and situations knowing what you and your mate could face, and plan ahead for how to divert the conversation, insert safe topics for discussion, or even have a code word that says, "Honey, I've had enough and I'm ready to go."

We know a couple who uses the word "cantaloupe" as a way of telling each other that they have had enough and need to leave.

Husband: "Wow, I'm really craving some cantaloupe."
Wife: "Oh yeah? I'll have to grab some from the store tomorrow."
(*To the others:*) "Well, it's been lovely having dinner with you all, but it's time for us to head out. Got to get the kids home and into bed, ya know."

This is why premarital counseling can be so helpful. We love to spend time with clients looking for potential "head off at the pass" opportunities.

The Bottom Line

Looking for opportunities to serve your mate, show you care, grow your marriage, and build a stronger home is common in healthy relationships. The opportunities present themselves daily if you pay attention to your mate, observe their body language, and hear what they're telling you—verbally and nonverbally.

And, you don't have to wait around for opportunities to do something helpful for your mate or to tell them how much they matter. Be intentional about creating those opportunities!

A LOOK IN THE MIRROR

1. How often do you study your mate to learn who they are?

2. In what ways are you your mate's #1 fan?

3. What was the last opportunity you had to support your mate? Did you do it?

4. Do you expect your mate to do something for you before you'll do something for them?

5. How can you use your next disagreement as an opportunity for growth?

6. What is one recurring, unpleasant situation you and your mate are subjected to? How can you limit discomfort or hurt feelings by preparing for such situation(s)?

7. What is one way you serve your mate in a way that's useful to them but not necessarily to you—for the betterment of the marriage?

PROTECT

—

To cover or shield from exposure, injury,
damage, or destruction; to maintain the
integrity of; to guard.

WHEN YOU THINK ABOUT PROTECTION, YOU MAY RUSH TO
thoughts of seatbelts, bike helmets, warning labels, notices that
we see every day, or even immunizations. Protection often comes with
those things, but the protection we're talking about is much more of a
mindset and series of choices than simply strapping on enough armor to
stave off the arrows from life's battles.

We'll let you in on a little secret that most people don't know about
us—something we found out about after we started dating. We both
love, love, love old black and white aviation disaster films! We stumbled
into a conversation about movies we loved as kids and why we loved
them. You would think it would have been *Towering Inferno, Willy Won-*
ka & The Chocolate Factory, or maybe even *Wizard of Oz* or *Smokey & The*
Bandit. Nope! Rather, it was movies like *Fate Is the Hunter, Zero Hour!,*
and *No Highway in the Sky*. Both of us remember watching these movies
as kids and being glued to the TV set. When we look back at what made
those so special to us, we can't help but believe it was seeing how the
combination of the smallest details in the story had such a devastating
impact on the outcome of the tragedy.

What Really Sunk the *Titanic?*

One of the areas within psychology that both of us find interesting is the area of organizational behavior, which is probably why we find working with couples so interesting. Like couples, organizations have a structure, culture, and framework that can lead to great success or devastating failure. We think those old black and white movies were an early awareness of both of our desires to understand the small nuances that led to disaster and the human element involved in discovering how to avoid them.

This is also what drives most of today's accident investigations. It's understanding the small and subtle influences that are placed in just the right order that result in life's tragedies. If you look back on any accident in history, you will see it's generally not the lack of protective equipment or the process that was at fault, but the combination of the right influences that came together at just the right time. Rarely, if ever, is it one thing. As we look at some of the greatest disasters in history, whether you're talking about the *Titanic* or the space shuttle *Challenger*, it wasn't just the iceberg that was struck or the O-rings that blew out. There was a host of other things on top of the one thing that led to disaster. This is also the same for marriages that fail. It's not just the affair or some final straw that breaks the back or sinks most marriages. It's often the small events, which can go unnoticed over time, that set the stage for what is perceived as the main event and the final blow.

The *Titanic* disaster didn't happen solely because of the design failures: the watertight doors that failed to go to the top of the ship, the rudder that was too small, the substandard steel plating, or even the problem with the rivets in the construction. It wasn't even the ship running at high speed in the flat, calm waters of well-known iceberg areas on a moonless night. We can't even say that it was the fault of the lookouts that didn't have the required binoculars. No, it wasn't just one of those that led to the greatest sea disaster in human history. It was all of them in concert.

The same is true in wildly successful relationships. It takes two engaged individuals to look at and relate to each other to ensure that they not only have the correct protective equipment, but also the awareness to see the bigger picture in the areas of relationship protection.

It's All About the Mindset

When we talk about protection in a marriage, we're not just talking about controlling what we do and don't do. Rather, it's about adopting a mindset that supports and defends the marriage across multiple fronts.

Without the mindset of protection, people can become complacent. And complacency can be dangerous. Complacent people put down their guard. They get comfortable. They take shortcuts. They get lazy. They get overconfident. Don't think that just because it hasn't happened yet, it can't happen one day. Stay vigilant.

Titanic was considered and advertised to be the unsinkable ship. They were so sure of this that they didn't even put enough lifeboats for the number of passengers aboard. They were that overconfident! And it ended disastrously—especially for the approximately 1,500 people who lost their lives when the ship went down.

Our point here is to never say never. Don't skip over the safety precautions just because you don't think you need them. Think of your marriage as your most important possession, one that must be guarded—without fail—daily. Keep a watchman's (or watchwoman's) eye out. Check the systems. Repairs the parts. Prepare the safety boats. Know your current position, your destination, and the waters you travel to get there. It's easy to let down your guard in the hustle and bustle of the day-to-day business and busyness, but those are precisely the times you miss the lurking and catastrophic icebergs.

We Protect the Things We've Invested In

We invest time, money, energy, and love in a lot of things. Because of that, we work hard to protect those things. When we care about something, we want to protect it. We want to keep it from harm, shelter it from damage, and put preventive measures in place to guard against those who could cause it harm. You wouldn't go on vacation and leave your house unlocked. If you're like most people, you have a checklist, either on paper or in your head. You check to make sure the windows are locked. You didn't leave the stove on, did you?

You pay your insurance premiums each year—just in case the unthinkable should happen to that home you built, furnished, and took care of. You're proud of your home. You want it to be protected: the furnishings you took such care to select; the appliances on which you rely; the family photos on the walls; that piece of artwork you paid too much for but bought anyway because your spouse really wanted it. You've become accustomed to all the beauty, functionality, and safety your home provides in your life. There's no way you'd leave all of that unprotected.

But, what about your marriage? It is by far your most important earthly relationship and should be of immeasurable worth and value to you. What do you do to protect it?

Installing Guardrails

Andy Stanley, in the *Guardrails for Marriage* series, puts a focus on putting up guardrails to keep you from potentially heading over the edge and off the cliff. He talks about the value and importance of warning systems. There are guardrails on the sides of roads, and Stanley encourages metaphoric guardrails in your marriage. He says, "In every area of our life where there is a desire, we need guardrails." In the area of our physical and sexual intimacy and desire for it, we need reinforced steel when it comes to guardrails.

Guardrails and walls are not meant to prevent you from having fun as you travel through life. Rather, they are there to help you get to your destination safely by protecting you when there is a dangerous curve, slippery spot, or a drop ahead.

Prevention as Protection

Protection isn't about waiting until something happens. It's also about putting systems in place to prevent problems before they arise. You don't buy insurance after you've wrecked the car. No, you purchase a policy that covers any potential damage. You hold a life insurance policy just in case (God forbid) the unthinkable happens. And you do that for protection. You protect your family.

Protection also means knowing your own thoughts and vulnerabilities. If you have night blindness, you avoid driving at night. When dieting, you don't bring the most tempting snacks and foods into the home. Or, as Joel says, "Don't go to Costco when you're hungry." (Anyone else guilty of doing this and regretting it?) Recognize your vulnerabilities and weaknesses. Then, put systems in place to manage or avoid them. Make sure you're protected.

> Recognize your vulnerabilities and weaknesses. Then, put systems in place to manage or avoid them.

As individuals and as a married couple, you have to take an honest look at yourselves. Ask the tough questions you might not like the answer to. What are my weaknesses? What tempts me the most? Where and how do my thoughts or eyes wander? Whatever those areas are, you need to have a plan for avoiding pitfalls and install guardrails to keep from devastation. A bump into a guardrail is a lot less costly than driving over a cliff.

Some couples identify their weakness as not spending enough time together. They lead busy lives or work opposite schedules. One couple, to protect their marriage and time together, may plan Saturday morning brunch dates every week. Another couple leaves love notes for each other to find throughout the week. While others will seek creative ways to stay connected.

A wife who recognizes her own insecurities might realize the man at the office who always flatters her is her weakness. So, she might guardrail herself by being transparent with her husband about the man and opting not to work with the co-worker on projects at work. Or a husband may admit that he's tempted by pornography and therefore asks his wife to install accountability software on his electronic devices.

It's not easy to admit that you have these weaknesses and temptations. You may even feel guilty about them. But failing to admit them and take appropriate precautions is failing to protect your marriage.

A Lesson in Castle Construction

In a signature talk that Kimberly gives, she uses the idea of castle walls to describe protection. If you're not familiar with castle construction (and we'd be surprised if you were!), imagine three rings that make up a series of castle walls. Each inner wall is successively smaller, with a courtyard separating each ring. Each provides a different level of protection. There can also be turrets and ramparts providing multiple levels of defense and maximizing the castle's defenses.

Think of the outer wall (exterior layer) as your first layer of defense. It is your first and most important line of defense. It should be thick and made of the strongest materials available. It should also be staffed with people to serve as lookouts, friendlies, and guards. These guards and lookouts are skilled. They have excellent vision and great aim in case they need to shoot arrows or throw rocks at the intruders.

Now, think in terms of your friends. Today, a group of close friends is often referred to as your tribe. These are your wingmen (or wingwomen or wing-persons—whatever you dub them). These are the friends that will tell it to you straight when you're in danger. These are also the people who will call you out should it be necessary. These are the people you rally when you need their protection and strength. They can be a type of fortress, metaphorically speaking.

Back to the castle. In this outer layer of protection, you will most likely have a moat and drawbridge. This is the gatekeeper's area. This is where you have systems in place to prevent people or things into your marriage that might do harm to it or undermine it—things that may weaken or even destroy it.

If your spouse has a history of betrayal, they might agree to make phone, computer, or bank info transparent. Passwords for social media accounts can be shared. There would be no secret accounts or email addresses. Maybe the 45-year-old man going through a midlife crisis decides not to hire a young, attractive secretary.

Because of these risk factors, this outer layer needs to be strong and invincible. If you were a castle attacker, would you go for the strong, fortified and heavily guarded one or the one in a state of disrepair? It's a rhetorical question. Of course, you might think that there is better stuff in the heavily fortified castle, but the easy target is where you would go. And this can be one of the reasons emotional affairs happen.

Emotional affairs usually start when one partner flirts or shares emotional or sensitive information with a third party, making you or your relationship seem vulnerable. This allows the intruder (albeit perhaps innocently) to slip right past that outer wall of defense because it's easy to breach.

In his book, *Anatomy of an Affair*, Dave Carder writes about the threats of seductive personalities, the risk factors you bring to your marriage, and the mood-altering potential of the Internet and digital friendships. The book analogizes protecting your marriage as putting hedges of protection around it and focusing on what is going on inside of you, not just the external behaviors.

Your next level of protection is more challenging and just as important to maintain than those outer walls. This level of protection, the inner level, includes people that you *have* to let in— perhaps friends or family members who make it past your initial outer defenses. Acquaintances and even some family members should have strictly lim-ited access to your inner circle if they undermine your relationship or immediate family. Think the sister-in-law who backchannels your kids, the co-worker who makes a pass at your husband, or a mother-in-law who gives your child snack food or soft drinks after you asked her not to. You might not want to use her as your primary babysitter. Your husband's cousin, who always flicks his cigarettes into your flower gar-den, should not be invited to your barbecue. You worked hard on those roses—how dare he have such disregard? These are the types of people who, simply by their close proximity to you, can compromise your for-tress. Their presence causes risk and stress factors that can weaken your castle walls.

Even though some people will make it past the first two levels of protection, you still have your inner, or personal, level of protection. This is where you store your reserves. This should be the safest level of all. It includes your beliefs and morals. It's where you keep your deepest hopes and dreams for a stronger marital relationship. It's where you keep your children, your closest family. And just like building a castle, building these relationships can take years—or even decades. Castles typically took from two to ten years to construct. Solid relationships, especially those with vulnerabilities needing protection, take time as well.

Your castle walls and our castle walls will be different. The dangers you need to fight off and protect your marriage from may be different than those threatening other marriages. Of course, there are some things we all want to guard ourselves from—those catastrophic blows such as infidelity. But every set of mates and every marriage is different. Their weaknesses and strengths differ. Their friendships and family dynamics differ. So, castle walls and defense mechanisms can vary—just make sure they are there!

Have a Strategy

This is all about prevention and setting your relationship up for success: protecting, safeguarding, intentionally planning your defenses, and executing such defenses as necessary. It's about treating your marriage as something more important than just momentary wants and desires or the individuals' wants and desires. Your relationship is valuable, and it is the job of both parties to protect the marriage, themselves, and their mate.

It's also about strategy—know your spouse and yourself very well and create a game plan. It takes work—every day, all day long.

Let's say your spouse is dyslexic. They should not be the go-to person for completing the kid's back-to-school paperwork. Why? Because this would put their vulnerability on display. That is not protecting. The same is true for other vulnerabilities. Karen stutters and highly stressful situations make the stuttering worse. Her husband, Jim, attends all the parent-teacher conferences, sometimes without her. He is shielding her. Knowing her sensitivity, he offered and has been *protecting* her ever since.

Use Only with Discretion

Protecting is also about using discretion. You shouldn't make fun of or tell others about your mate's dreams or secret wishes. You wouldn't tell people or broadcast in a social media group if your mate has ED or had an affair. You don't belittle your mate, either. Don't share secrets with buddies about what your wife is like in bed, whether complaining because she is too vanilla or bragging that you are swinging off the chandeliers each night. And never, ever compare your mate to an ex—good or bad. You are your mate's confidant and marriage protector.

A good strategy some couples take is to have your spouse's interests and needs as the first item on your list of things to protect. Your spouse, in turn, has your interests and needs as the first thing on their list. Couples who practice this know that whatever their partner does is always about protecting them, and vice versa. And, as time goes on, it becomes automatic. You know that they have your back, and they know that you have theirs—100% of the time. This level of protection is about complete trust in your partner's intentions and can be difficult for some couples to achieve. Remember jumping into the pool as a kid, with dad promising to catch you? At first, you were scared to try. But after the first time he caught you, you knew he meant to keep his word. He wasn't going to let you get hurt. His only focus in that pool was protecting you and making sure you were safe.

Remember, your marriage should be a safe space, too. It's your grand castle—built with care and purpose. Your life together, and the path on which you set forth, are yours and only yours. It is a sacred space, fragile and worthy of protection.

The Bottom Line

We protect that which is most valuable to us. What could be of more value than our marriages? We protect our marriages from internal and external attacks by being aware of our areas of weakness and making a plan for safeguarding against them. Just as castles were erected to protect the kingdom and its important members, we surround ourselves with safety nets and layers of protection. And we guard our marriages by using accountability, planning, and intentionality.

A LOOK IN THE MIRROR

1. Besides your marriage, what are some things you protect?

2. Why might people fail to protect their marriages?

3. What guardrails do you and your mate have in place now to safeguard your marriage?

4. What areas of weakness have you left exposed and vulnerable?

5. Who in your life serves as a lookout or first layer of defense for your castle?

6. In our ever-changing, digital world, how do you and your mate protect yourselves and each other?

7. Have you ever witnessed a mate fail to use discretion? How would it make you feel if you were the mate being exposed?

QUIETING

—

To silence, still, and calm; to make less noisy,
less active, or less busy.

SOME OF OUR FRIENDS WHO LOVE PUZZLES ARE INTO THOSE ANA-gram games as well. An anagram is where you make words from the letters of another word. One of our favorite anagrams has made its way around the web. It's the social media meme that illustrates how the words "listen" and "silent" use the same letters. Maybe you've seen it? Or maybe you're just now realizing this. It's okay—our minds were blown by this, too. And we like to think it's quite a happy coincidence. Either way, it's a great reminder that being a good listener sometimes requires us to be silent—or just quiet.

Just as there is value in communication and listening, there is value in quieting. Most people, however, are not good listeners, in large part due to our inability to quiet our thoughts. It is rare to have been taught to be a good listener. We are often too focused on planning for our response, which makes it difficult to be a good listener.

Stephen Covey, in *The 7 Habits of Highly Effective People,* says, "Most people do not listen with the intent to understand; they listen with the intent to reply." This is true in marriages, too. When we listen with only the intent to respond, we're missing out on valuable information, and, sadly, we hinder effective communication as a result. Effective listening is quieting the mind so as to be able to listen and learn—listening so your mate feels heard. To listen is to make a connection. To listen is to gain a fuller understanding. And to listen is to be quiet.

Quieting is Slowing

Quieting is a form of slowing. It is slowing down your thoughts, your actions, your impulses, and your reactions. It is being more deliberate in responses rather than reacting impulsively. The movie *The Vow* is a great example of the value of slowing. The lead female character (played by Rachel McAdams) has lost her memory due to a car accident and the lead male (played by Channing Tatum) is trying to help her be back to her old self. In one scene, rather than being deliberate in their responses to one another, McAdams' character snaps at Tatum and he retorts, "I'm trying to help you, but I'm not your punching bag. We don't speak to each other like this."

In successful relationships, there are two important types of quieting that couples practice. The first is being quiet (discerning) when things are heated, rather than saying something that cannot be taken back. That is what McAdams' and Tatum's characters show us in the movie. And the second is quieting to listen to internal thoughts so that one can more fully understand—and later communicate—the depths and authenticity of what we're feeling.

It can be a challenge to slow down and to be quiet. In heated conversations or heightened emotional states, our amygdala (a part of our brain that plays a role in emotions) gets hijacked and wants to take over. We have physiological responses that result in hormones getting pumped into our autonomic nervous systems. In concert, cortisol, glucagon, epinephrine, norepinephrine, and other chemicals start surging through our systems and activating our fight-or-flight response. And it takes time for the chemicals to subside. Taking a long shower or bath, exercising, taking a long walk, or even sleeping can help buy time to get the chemicals to quiet down. An even better approach is to quiet or slow down before the surge of chemicals can be dumped into your system, which prevents them from impacting you.

Quieting may seem awkward or even abnormal if you grew up in a household with frequent yelling, arguing, and loud environments or if you've developed a habit in your current relationships where there are lots of outbursts and door-slamming scenarios. At the very least, quieting will feel unfamiliar. Learning not to just blurt out impulsively whatever you want to say is imperative.

Quieting is not to be confused with giving someone the silent treatment. Quieting is not a form of manipulation, avoidance, or punishment. Again, we're not talking about "the silent treatment". Quieting is the reflective and thoughtful treatment.

Further, quiet listening (sometimes called active listening) means that when quieting, you don't keep looking away in distraction, don't sigh as if bored, and don't roll your eyes as a sign of disapproval or irritation. Quiet listening is attentive listening. Research repeatedly shows that eye contact when listening, along with affirmative actions like the occasional nod, helps the person feel more understood and listened to.

Quieting the Internal

Learning to regularly quiet internal chatter is good in all areas of life. It allows us to think and understand before we respond, enabling us to respond more effectively and authentically than just reacting. We should become quick to quiet, slow to judge, and even slower to respond when times are intense or heated.

Doug was previously married to what most would describe as a hothead. Doug's previous wife was sure to let him know when she was disappointed in him, his actions, and inactions, usually with expletives. June, Doug's current wife, is quieter about her feelings. Doug was attracted to her even-keeled nature, but also found her quiet moments unsettling. He even feared that if they ever argued, she would be quick to leave him. So, when June got quiet and contemplative, he called it "going dark". He always felt "on the ready" for June to throw down an ultimatum. It took years for Doug to get used to June quieting. After her quieting time, June always approaches Doug to talk about what's been on her mind, and then they can work together to understand and resolve any problems.

Maybe you have heard the adage that each time we say hurtful things to our mate, it's like hammering a nail in the fence. Our 'apologies' are the acts of taking the nail out of the fence. But the nail hole—an injury—remains. Successful couples work to slow their thoughts, comments, and what they say to minimize or even prevent most nail holes in their relationship. Many of our clients will say things out of anger or being upset and justify what was said in the heat of the moment, only to regret it later. "Well, he just needs to ignore me when I'm like that," or "She knows that I didn't mean it." Here's the rub: What you said in the heat of the moment cannot be unsaid and taken back. The nail cannot be 'un-nailed' without leaving a scar. It's out there, and it stays with your mate and potentially with others when said in public or around children. Saying later that you didn't mean it still leaves you with a nail hole that weakens the fence.

How many nail holes are in your relationship? How many can it take before it is too weak to stand up against a strong breeze?

Truth in the Stereotypes?

Each couple makes up their own unique relationship, but there still seems to be some stereotypes that often hold true.

Problem Solver

More often than not, men want to solve problems. They can be prone to listening with the intent to solve. And, while they're in a rush to solve, their mate may feel less than understood. Have you seen the viral video, "It's Not About the Nail"? It's a prime example of one partner just wanting to vent and feel heard, and the other wanting to solve the problem. Neither is wrong, but they're still having problems.

Flight or Freeze

Another stereotype that can be misunderstood is the quieting that men often do. When faced with an affront, the response can be fight, flight, or freeze. Not wanting to "fight" with their mate, men can get quiet or leave. Women will interpret this as not caring, but in some cases a man may perceive walking away to be their best option. Or they may "freeze" by not interacting, rather than fighting, with their mate. Some may see this as stonewalling, while many men that do this, may actually be trying their best to respect their partner but not engaging into a fight.

Nagging

Likewise, a common complaint that we hear from men about their wives is nagging. Let's understand nagging a bit better. Oftentimes, when a woman is perceived to be nagging, it's misinterpreted because it might take quieting time to fully understand what she's feeling. Women "nag" primarily for two reasons: One, she has asked for something that has been stewing in the back of her head and needs to get resolved—like checking it off a list. Not having it done is stressing her because it's taking up valuable mental bandwidth. Two, she feels unappreciated.

Andrea does the laundry in her house, meaning sorting, washing, folding, and putting it on everyone's dressers. After that, each family member deals with their own laundry by putting it into drawers or hanging it up. When laundry sits on dressers and is not put away promptly, it bothers Andrea—not because she's a control freak, but because she feels unappreciated. Andrea works hard to care for her family. And deep down, she wants them to appreciate her efforts; in this case, it means the final step in the process of laundry. She noticed that when her family heaped praise on her for the clean clothes, she was less likely to be bothered by the clothes still sitting on the dresser a few days later.

Just a Difference of Opinion

Sometimes there is just a difference of opinion on the proper way to do

> Do not bully your mate into agreement or assume they're wrong for not seeing it your way.

something. As you will read more than once in this book, we contend that a different approach or method does not necessarily equal a wrong approach or method. This is where listening (quieting) to understand is important. But understanding does not always equal agreement. Nor does understanding lead to agreement. Do not bully your mate into agreement or assume they're wrong for not seeing it your way.

Set for Success

Quieting is a great time to ask internally and authentically, "What do I hope to get out of this conversation with my mate?" Is it just a utilitarian data dump of information? If so, maybe it is best communicated via a note, text, or email so they can refer back to it if needed.

If you've ever watched a debate between politicians on news shows, you've likely noticed that they each try to dominate the conversation in an effort to drown out others or prevent them from their turn altogether. Couples in conflict can be prone to this pattern, too. This is broadcast bullying and does not lead to effective communication.

Also, for difficult conversations, it may be best to have shorter conversations rather than both of you repeating yourselves, making each other feel bullied and beat up. A well-thought-out topic should be easy to communicate clearly and succinctly—in less than 10 minutes. Be sure to offer your partner quiet time to reflect on a topic before revisiting. If you're in a race to resolve an issue, you may do more damage than if you just took things slower.

Ellen is understandably hurt after Chuck had an affair. She says that she wants to save the marriage, but she is deeply hurt and afraid. Chuck says that Ellen takes every opportunity to remind him of his violation, following him around the house, talking at him, and reminding him how hurt she is. They both agree that this can go on for hours at night.

If your quieting time reveals something you need to communicate with your mate, something heavy on your heart, or your fears or concerns, then set up your mate for success so you can have a positive resolution. There are three ways you can help that happen:

- **Seek to have difficult conversations rather than difficult situations.** While difficult conversation can still leave nail holes in a fence, the nail holes they leave can be equated to a small finish nail compared to the railroad spike hole that other acts of indiscretions leave.

- **Gauge the scene.** Consider the timing, the location, your energy level and your mate's, and more before you tackle a tough topic.

- **Do not expect your mate to agree just because they say they understand.** If you do not agree with your mate, consider the phrase, "Help me understand".' It is a powerful phrase, but it's also a request that requires one to be quiet and listen; to understand rather than to respond or coerce.

What Quieting is NOT

You can't take time to quiet your actions, listen intently to your mate's words for understanding, examine your own feelings, and prepare a response rather than a reaction if you're doing one of the following:

- Posting some rant session on Facebook in hopes of getting feedback.
- Texting with your friends to drum up support.
- Calling your mom or bestie to complain about your mate.

This is not quieting. It's triangulating. And this is not protecting your marriage or respecting your mate.

The Bottom Line

Quiet isn't just an adjective to describe no noise, but also a verb where we take specific actions to quiet ourselves (internally and externally).

Quieting means that we slow our reactions so we can best respond when needed. It means actively listening to our mates rather than listening to respond.

Famous financial and political advisor Bernard M. Baruch once said, "Most of the successful people I've known are the ones who do more listening than talking." This could easily be applied to and adapted for successful marriages, too. When we do more listening to our mates than talking *at* them, we help build a thriving marriage and a mate who feels heard, understood, and loved. And who could ask for more than that?

A LOOK IN THE MIRROR

1. How well do you and your mate actually listen to one another?

2. How can you show your mate that you are actively listening rather than listening to respond?

3. What's the difference between quieting ourselves vs. giving the silent treatment?

4. Do you tend to respond to a tense conversation with the fight, flight, or freeze response? What about your mate?

5. How can you set up your mate for success when you need to discuss a tough topic?

6. What does quieting realistically look like for you when you put it into practice?

7. Why is listening just as much a part of communication as speaking?

REGULATION

One's ability to interact and stay emotionally and logically connected with themselves and others during times of fear, stress, and conflict.

F OR THOSE OF YOU WITH CHILDREN, DID YOU READ ALL OF THOSE *What to Expect When You're Expecting* books? These books have served as great resources for expectant parents-to-be. One of the chapters covers what to expect the first few days and weeks after a baby is born. Fascinatingly enough, the book teaches that a baby's heart rate and body temperature can better regulate themselves when they are being held and cuddled by their parents in the moments, days, and weeks following birth. After nine months in the womb, cuddling close outside of the womb helps soothe the baby—especially when they can feel mom's heartbeat again. Hospitals are now actively encouraging immediate skin-to-skin contact between parents and babies so as to help with the regulation of these systems.

As we grow and mature, there are other ways our bodies regulate themselves, and sometimes, we need to take intentional measures to help do this, particularly in highly charged mental and emotional states. In this element, we want to talk about some of the reasons that regulation is so important and why it is such a vital part of a wildly successful relationship.

Regulation is about having the ability to self-soothe and control one's emotional state when one is feeling compelled to fight, flight, or freeze due to some heightened emotional state from. Everyone is capable of regulating their emotions to some degree or another, or else nothing would get done in this world. In this element, what we aim to do is increase your awareness of the significance and enormous value of emotional regulation.

Emotional regulation plays a big role in thriving marriages, and it's closely related to other elements in this book such as awareness, knowledge, and understanding. Like many of the others, emotional regulation is part of the theme of being attuned to ourselves and one another.

How Wide is Your River?

Nothing beats a great word picture to explain things, so let us try to illustrate for you the value of emotional regulation. Think of emotional regulation as a river you are traveling down on a raft.

On one bank of the river, you have seemingly calm water up against a steep bank, but in reality there are small snags and hidden objects lurking just below the surface. On the other side, you have rough waters due to a host of visible sharp rocks and varying sized obstacles. Neither bank of the river feels like a secure place for you to be for fear of damaging your relationship raft. Thus, the goal is to stay away from both banks and float safely in the middle.

Let's identify the steep banked side with the hidden snags and submerged objects as being emotionally shut down (hypo-emotional). The bank with the obvious sharp rocks and dangerous objects represents being overwhelmed and chaotic (hyper-emotional).

The width of the river represents the degree of one's emotional regulation. A wide river is ideal. For some, however, their emotional regulation is narrow and little more than a seasonal stream. They spend much of their time bouncing off the banks, vacillating between being overly chaotic and under engaged.

The idea of staying in the middle of the river borrows from the work and book by Dan Siegel and Tina Payne Bryson: *The Whole Brain Child*.

In the book, they explain that the chaotic side is marked by confusion and described as being messy and disorganized. The other side is marked by being uncompromising and overcontrolling. Siegal also gave us the metaphor of the 'Window of Tolerance' with the key terms of hyper-arousal (overwhelm, panic, fight, or flight) and hypo-arousal (numb, depressed, unmotivated, frozen). The goal is to stay within a range (the Window of Tolerance) and also continually widen it. A wide Window of Tolerance allows one to respond thoughtfully and skillfully to difficult emotions and situations. Likewise, a wide river of emotional regulation lets people stay on the relational journey without shifting too far to one side or the other. They stay off the banks and don't resort to chaos (hyper-emotion) or shutting down (hypo-emotion), both of which limit one's ability to stay engaged. Regardless of the metaphor, the goal is the same: Stay away from the extremes.

The Science Behind It

In neurobiology, the river of emotional regulation is a very real thing and speaks to how the human mind functions and processes information. When we become deregulated, there's something physically taking place in the brain. Two major systems that need to communicate with one another are temporarily tripping offline, meaning that the connection between one's feelings and one's logic is greatly reduced, if not disconnected altogether (temporarily).

To simplify, the human brain needs these two major systems working together to solve a complex problem. The emotional system of our brain is the limbic system, and you will often hear us call it our "Emotional Rolodex". It keeps track of all kinds of past experiences—many of which we may not even remember verbally or consciously. It's also known as the fast-acting part of our brain and often has a primed response that drives most of our daily tasks and interactions.

The other part of the brain is the cerebral cortex, which—for simplicity—we'll call the "Simulator" because it's able to simulate a reality (real or not). This is the part of the brain that lets us create things that have never been. We can thank the cerebral cortex for artists, musicians, architects, etc., because it's what helps create things like music, stories, art, and more. It's also what helps create relationships.

Emotions (thanks to the limbic system) are important because without them, we have no ability to relate to others. Likewise, logic and thought (thanks to the cerebral cortex) are important because we can't imagine, create, or maintain relationships without them. The fascinating part about these two systems is that they can regulate and deregulate one another. It's critical to understand how the systems work and that everyone can benefit from regulation. It's a key factor one needs to create and maintain in a wildly successful marriage.

The Ying and the Yang

People often ask, "Do your emotions drive your thoughts or do your thoughts drive your emotions?" The short answer is, "YES!" They both can and do impact and affect each other. The great thing is that once you understand the relationship between the two of them, you can widen your own river of emotional regulation and stay off the banks.

Someone once said, "Emotions are like children! We don't let them drive the car, but you can't keep them in the trunk either!" To widen your own river of emotional regulation, you need to be able to start looking *at* your emotions rather than *through* them. We need to recognize that feelings and emotions are important. We need to understand and examine them, but they cannot be our singular source of motivation. Too many of us let our emotions color our view of the world, much like wearing tinted lenses affects how we see objects. It's not just *what* you're feeling emotionally but also *why* you're feeling that way—and what that *causes* you to do or not do as a result.

The Aftermath of Emotions

Our emotions are also tied to a third part of our brain—the brainstem, the interface between brain and body. It controls many of our bodily functions that require no conscious thought, like our body's temperature and circulation.

Much of our emotional responses have a physical reaction. If we're stressed, maybe our stomachs turn into knots, our hearts begin to race, or our palms become sweaty. We can often have a physical awareness of our emotions when we're nearing one of the banks. A wide river affords us time to think and feel and thus allows for course correction before it is too late—before we are left with a tangled or disabled raft. Being aware of and understanding their own limitations allows ample time for most people to make course corrections (via actions or thoughts) to avoid the dangerous banks of the river.

If you practice and make the effort, then over time you'll be better able to increase your awareness of what you're feeling. This is how you widen your river—or at least know you're becoming emotionally flooded before you hit the banks. You'll have a heads up that no good thing will come unless you can assess any damage, bail out any water, and get back in the middle of the river.

Let Your Mate In

Each time you work to grow your awareness, authentically communicate, and make your thinking more visible to your partner, you are building the level of understanding between the two of you. And greater understanding leads to greater empathy and intimacy in your marriage. You are helping your mate know where you are emotionally at that moment and where you're headed.

It is important to be able to feel and respond to emotions. Your emotions are the reason you can attune to others and have empathy. You are capable of understanding and feeling what it must be like for your mate to experience what they are experiencing. (Reread that sentence because we know it was a tongue twister.) The goal is to embrace your emotions while also avoiding being overly emotional. Conversely, some people are severely lacking in emotions and can therefore dismiss others' feelings. They sometimes seem to have an inability to feel or understand what others are experiencing, coming off as apathetic or even heartless. The sweet spot is somewhere in the middle.

When Your Rivers Are Different

Nancy often feels that Dale doesn't care and is always dismissing her feelings. She regularly becomes angry when she feels he's withdrawing from her; and typically, she'll respond out of frustration, blaming him for not caring or accusing him of not loving her. Dale perceives this as anger. He feels that Nancy is too emotional and can't see the forest for the trees. He thinks she's always flipping out and making too big of a deal of things. "You know, not everything's an emergency, Nancy!" Of course, this only makes her feel misunderstood and that much more distant from Dale.

What's going on between Nancy and Dale is sadly all too common with couples. Each is struggling with a different aspect of regulation. Due to years of feeling dismissed and misunderstood, Nancy's perceptions cause her to lean towards hypersensitivity. She's almost always ready and primed to find fault and accuse Dale of not caring. Dale's perception of her causes him to be unwilling to let her feel understood, and that has worked against him, draining Nancy's emotional regulation river to a seasonal stream. Her inability to regulate her emotions has worked against her, too, causing Dale to drift further away from her. Each one affects the other's perception of who they are, thereby working in concert to drive co-created negative patterns between them.

Again, the key here is to better understand how and why we need to regulate our emotions and how that will impact your partner. We are all faced with endless limitations, and no one person sees things the same as the other. Working to manage your regulation and widen your river is very much a critical factor that can't be overlooked in relationships.

Taking Control

Emotional dysregulation happens. And everyone has circumstances in which they are more prone or susceptible to becoming unregulated. Whatever the reason for the emotional dysregulation, it is important to recognize when you or your partner are out of the flow of the river (or Window of Tolerance) and drifting towards the dangerous banks. The most successful marriages are found in couples in which both parties are willing to own and take charge of their emotional regulation. It is each of your responsibilities to work to get back to the center of the stream and into smoother waters.

Another metaphor that we use to explain emotional regulation involves a thermostat with hot or cold extremes that represent hyper-emotional and hypo-emotional states. If you are cold, you can add layers of clothing, come in from the cold, turn up the heat, get physically moving to get your blood pumping, and/or drink something warm to avoid the chill and prevent hypothermia. Likewise, if overheated one could take steps to cool down and prevent heat exhaustion.

Deciding to take responsibility for your emotional temperature is the crucial first step. And it starts with being aware. Aware of situations, options, circumstances, physical states, even people that cause you to drift towards one side or the other. Learning how to recognize when you or your partner are headed for dysregulation and being equipped to regulate your own emotions will help keep you in the middle of the emotional river (or thermostat), and thus prevent you from shutting down or becoming flooded.

Let's be very clear here: those who struggle but fail to regulate their emotions are likely doing harm to their relationships. Honestly, it may cause severe and potentially irreparable harm. These people are going to need to put in the individual work to address their unique situation before they will see significant improvements in their relationship.

One of the most self-empowering steps you can take, not only for yourself but also for the health of your relationship, is to understand and accept that you're in charge of your emotions. No one makes you feel what you feel. The moment you let others dictate your emotional state you give away a tremendous amount of personal power. We advocate that everyone needs to take personal responsibility for their emotions, but we humbly acknowledge it is easier said than done. Taking ownership of your own emotional state, however, positions you for repairing the past and also preventing or reducing future problems. And who doesn't want that?

How that is achieved and what that looks like will clearly differ from person to person and from couple to couple. Counseling to heal past traumas and personal associations may be needed for some, while others' solutions may lie in a deep look at chemical or hormonal imbalances including blood sugar levels, hydration, physical fitness, and sleep hygiene. Physical processes greatly impact the ability to regulate emotions. Never underestimate them. While we typically do not rush to medication as a solution, we know that for some it may be necessary.

A successful marriage is realized when you and your mate are accountable to each other regarding those periods of deregulation. Become aware of when it's likely to happen and why, and then take positive action(s) to help each other—not only to stay in the middle of the river but also to widen it.

The Bottom Line

We are naturally wired with the ability to respond emotionally, logically, or a combination of both. Without emotional regulation you are left adrift to bounce off the banks of your emotional river, resulting in

> Having the ability to understand and regulate your emotions is key.

being emotionally overwhelmed or emotionally shut down.

Having the ability to understand and regulate your emotions is key. Knowing your tendencies and proclivities helps you take actions to adjust your course and to consistently work to widen your emotional river. For example, does your emotional river get narrower when you're sleepy or hungry? What about when you're dealing with work deadlines or faced with a previous hurt? Likely, your answer is yes. After all, you are human.

Further, knowing your mate's emotional tendencies and communicating yours to them helps bring a level of understanding and empathy into your relationship. You can then help steer one another to a more neutral state and better tackle whatever conflict or obstacle is at hand. It will also help your mate to feel more known and loved by you—which is a very beneficial component in a wildly successful marriage.

When you can take wise and thoughtful preventive and corrective actions, you're able to keep your Rolodex and Simulator from disconnecting. Ideally, that will keep you off the banks of your emotional river, avoiding the potential of damaging your relationship. The great news is that emotional regulation gets easier with awareness, thoughtfulness, and practice.

A LOOK IN THE MIRROR

1. How wide is your emotional river? Is it more like a creek or the Mississippi River?

2. What about your mate? Do they tend to respond more logically or emotionally?

3. How do your emotional differences cause you to relate to one another in conflict?

4. What is one way you know your mate is deregulated?

5. What is one way you know you're deregulated?

6. What is one way your mate can help steer your raft back into the middle of the emotional river? What is one way you can help them in return?

7. What is one advantage to being able to respond emotionally in relationships? What is one advantage of responding more logically?

SAFETY

—

Freedom from danger, risk, or injury.

NYCTINASTY [NYC·TI·NAS·TY] IS A MECHANISM THAT ALLOWS A plant to respond to day and night cycles as well as temperature changes. It is a tactical movement of certain flowers like the California Poppy, Daisy, and Morning Glory, in which they can open and close throughout the day and night. You've probably seen this before. But why would a plant benefit from this? Well, being able to open during the day allows their petals to absorb a maximum amount of sunlight. Closing at night allows them to protect themselves from unwanted pests as well as frost and cooler temperatures. It conserves the plants' energies for the daytime when pollinators are most active.

These flowers operate in a manner that gets them to fully open up and show their beauty when they feel safest—which is during the day for these particular flowers.

You cannot have trust, hope, and intimacy, nor can you feel free to embrace resolving conflict, without a sense of safety in a relationship. It is when we feel safe to honestly communicate and safe to explore our deepest hopes, dreams, and desires that we can grow closer and achieve a deeper connection and intimacy with others.

Safety in a relationship is often only thought of as a sense of being physically safe. And physical safety is absolutely crucial in a successful relationship. We contend, however, that safety in a relationship boils down to three generalized areas, including physical safety, but not limited to physical safety. All three elements of safety are necessary to create a thriving relationship.

Physical Safety

Physical safety is the most obvious type of safety in a relationship. Basically, if anyone is hitting, pushing, kicking, or using any kind of physical force in a relationship, it's dangerous. And unacceptable. Sexual abuse and throwing things at your partner are forms of physical abuse and are never acceptable—under ANY circumstances.

Domestic violence is a serious issue. A recent study showed that an average of three women a day are killed by their partners in the United States. Of all the women murdered each year, about a third of them were killed by their partners.

Sadly, it is not only women who face violence at the hands of an intimate partner. One in seven men annually report some form of severe physical abuse from their intimate partners. Women tend to use weapons or throw things more than men in domestic violence. Some of this is in response to previous violence against them, but not all. And abuse perpetrated by women on their mates has increased. In general, men do more damage, and women use objects.

Without blaming one gender or the other, let's just say that it is never okay for men OR women to use physical violence to abuse or harm a partner—or anyone else. If you or your partner are having problems with anger and/or experiencing physical safety concerns, please reach out and seek professional help immediately. Do not wait. Whether a man or woman, if you are physically afraid that your mate will become violent, then please seek professional help right away.

Abuser or abused? It is not always clear which is which, and abuse can cause a victim to abuse back, creating a horrible cycle. Follow the case of Johnny Depp and Amber Heard and their abuse allegations. It is a sordid mess of "he said/she said". Yes, sometimes people make false claims of abuse. But each case should be taken very seriously. I (Kimberly) had a client admit that she had made a false claim to police that her boyfriend hit her when he actually hadn't. She said she wanted to get him arrested because he was kicking her out of his house. She also admitted to frequently blocking the door when he would try to leave during an argument and daring him to hit her. These actions are unacceptable. And illegal.

Fear for physical safety from a partner is a considerable barrier to communication, honesty, trust, and engagement, all of which are necessary for a successful relationship. If you're fearful for your safety, it's completely understandable that you'd be uninterested in openly and honestly sharing your thoughts and feelings. In fact, trying to communicate these things might put you in danger. You would very likely (and understandably) go into self-protection mode, hiding your feelings and wants.

Most adults who are physically (and sexually) abusive were themselves abused by someone close: a family member, a mate, a neighbor, etc. The saying rings true that "Hurt people, hurt people".

Emotional Safety

It's harder to get people to agree on a definition of emotional abuse than a definition of physical abuse. In fact, the term 'emotional abuse' gets thrown around quite a lot in our practice. We agree that emotional abuse happens, but we can't always agree with clients on its definition.

For example, arguing and even yelling at your partner does not necessarily constitute emotional abuse. It depends on how the two partners view this kind of arguing, which is generally a result of previous life experiences. Belittling, name calling, ridiculing, and harshly criticizing your mate could easily fall under emotional abuse. Shaming, blaming, and openly criticizing your mate in front of others could also fall under emotional abuse. But they may not always. Moreover, people raised in a large family with loud arguments might feel that arguing loudly does not mean there is a lack of love. For others, getting yelled at during childhood meant physical abuse was on the way, so a loud argument could be terrifying. Or, understandably, they might be more sensitive to arguing if voices are raised.

A client named Dan shared in session that he thought his wife didn't love him because she walked away from him every time there was an argument. He later came to understand that she had very different reactions to loud arguments than he did based on previous experiences. Our past experiences tint how we see behavior—the behavior is not necessarily right or wrong.

Some clients claim emotional abuse for things like their mate disagreeing with them, refusing to do a specific activity with them, or denying them something they wanted. Tawna and her husband were saving to buy a new car, and they had agreed to set aside a specific amount each month to save for a large down payment. Tawna decided that she wanted to take some of the money from the car savings and buy a new couch. Bill, her husband, refused to go along with the new couch idea, and Tawna said that his refusal to even talk about it was emotional abuse. The refusal may not have been the healthiest response, but we disagree that it was emotional abuse. Further, Tawna has a habit of being impulsive with money, and that is why it takes both of them to withdraw money. The solutions were to help Tawna understand her behaviors, motivations, and needs, and to teach them both another way to communicate and compromise.

Maybe you are considered "hypersensitive" due to past abuse(s) or abandonment issues. Being *hypersensitive* does not make you wrong. It just means that you and your partner have to work harder to understand and build trust and safety. But it is worth it.

Real emotional abuse happens! When one partner attempts to control another through deception or other overt actions, they are dabbling in emotional abuse. It may be severe criticism, changing the rules constantly, or intentionally doing things to make the partner feel off kilter.

You've probably heard the term gaslighting. This is when one partner does and says things to make it look as if the other partner is crazy or mentally unstable. The term gaslighting comes from the dark 1944 George Cukor film in which the lead male (Charles Boyer) gets the lead female (Ingrid Bergman) to doubt her own sanity as he isolates her in their old house. He intentionally moves or removes things and turns the gas lamps up and down behind her back, treating her as if she imagined the changes. That's a form of emotional abuse.

Emotional abuse is also calling your mate names for expressing themselves rather than honestly trying to understand and help them sort out their feelings and the depths of them, criticizing your mate, male or female, for having feelings and emotions. It's teasing or ridiculing your mate for sexual performance or physical attributes, or even telling your friends things that your partner told you in private. People have insecurities, so resist cheap jabs and criticism on a known weakness or sensitivity.

Throwing around the term "emotional abuse" and claiming a victim role with the intention of getting your way is tantamount to a toddler throwing a tantrum on the floor of the grocery store because they want a specific cereal. Toxic relationships do this.

Relationship Safety

Relationship safety might sound much like emotional safety, but relationship safety is critically different. The difference lies in the safety of the relationship itself—the partnership.

Relationship safety violations happen when one partner acts as if they are prepared to end the relationship at any moment. Consider it to be threatening to use the "scorched earth" option. Visualize it this way: One partner has poured gas on the floor and is standing there with a lit match. And if the other partner doesn't do exactly as the first partner wishes, the first partner is threatening to drop the match and burn it all down.

Fear that the relationship is on the verge of doom paralyzes the second partner, who feels as if they are about to be left at any moment for any small mistake or lapse. Figuratively, they are being held hostage. It prevents them from being authentic, prohibits honest communication, and stunts the growth of the relationship.

If you believe that the slightest disagreement can cause your mate to stop loving you and leave, your willingness to have those difficult—but necessary—discussions can drop to zero. It can keep you frozen in fear.

Lynda used to keep a bag packed at the door for her kids and herself. She did it to reinforce the idea that she could leave her husband, Kyle, at any moment. This went on for years, and it took its toll on their marriage. Lynda said that she wanted Kyle to appreciate her and realize that she didn't have to stay. She thought it was good for him.

Ladies who are reading this, take note. One of your husband's greatest fears is that you will leave him and take the kids, too. He likely won't tell you this, but we can and will, because we've had countless men tell us this.

Everyone has a breaking point. After 15 years of marriage, Kyle recently filed for divorce and asked for primary custody of their kids. He explained that he didn't want his ex-wife to pack the kids' bags and kick them out or subject them to her conditional love approach.

Lynda was shocked when Kyle packed his *own* bags and left her, refusing to discuss reconciliation. For years, she had abused the relationship by holding desertion over Kyle's head. This is just as destructive to the relationship as emotionally or physically abusing your partner. If you don't have relationship safety, you're not able to be yourself. You don't feel safe to express your wants, hopes, dreams, and desires, nor are you safe to be imperfect and flawed or to grow and evolve.

> Life and marriages have wind gusts and downdrafts. We need altitude to allow for recovery time in these cases.

Relationship safety can also be visualized as a low-flying plane that is skimming the treetops. With the plane flying so low, there is no room for course correction or rebounding after a wind gust or air pocket. Thus, a patch of bad weather forces the plane (your relationship) into the trees because you don't have the altitude needed to gain the necessary lift. Where there is no altitude over the trees, there is no margin (confidence) in the relationship.

Life and marriages have wind gusts and downdrafts. We need altitude to allow for recovery time in these cases. Confidence and safety in your relationship means that it can withstand an air pocket because the subsequent 100-foot drop won't drive you into the ground.

Other Safety Concerns

Your mate may be participating in some behaviors that are risky to your family's safety and well-being. Addictions like substance abuse can risk your physical safety for a variety of reasons—mood swings, inability to operate a vehicle safely, etc. Similarly, addictions like gambling can pose a risk to your emotional and relational safety because your mate is probably lying repeatedly about where they are or where your finances are going. Sexual addictions pose a threat to your safety, too. If your mate is struggling with a sexual addiction, there's a physical risk of disease transmission as well as the more obvious risks to your emotional and relationship safety. Any of the above situations would best be addressed and treated by a professional. While you cannot force your mate to seek help, you can and should seek safety for yourself.

Finally, when addressing any of the three elements of safety with your mate, take a look at the intent of your partner. Did they intend to inhibit communication or trust? Were they knowingly undermining the relationship? Or was it an unintentional repercussion of behavior? A lot of safety really comes down to whether your mate has good intentions towards you. When we're working with a couple, we often ask, "Do you believe he/she meant to hurt you?" The answer to this is very telling. A spouse who says they feel emotionally unsafe but also believes their mate didn't intend to make them feel that way may actually be having issues communicating, understanding, and practicing awareness with their mate.

The Bottom Line

People need all three types of safety—physical, emotional, and relational—to feel safe in a relationship; only then can it be healthy enough that the relationship and both people in it can thrive. Without safety, you live in a degree of fear, and the healthy components of the relationship can't survive. You can't trust. You can't love. You can't communicate well, and you can't relax. Eventually, the relationship gets as weakened as a home with termite infestation.

A LOOK IN THE MIRROR

1. Do you feel safe with your mate—physically and emotionally?

2. Do you experience relationship safety with your mate?

3. Would your mate say he/she is emotionally and physically safe with you?

4. Have you ever done anything to jeopardize your mate's feelings of safety in the relationship?

5. What are some ways you've seen others abuse their mates emotionally or relationally?

6. How do the three elements of safety work together to help you and your mate thrive?

7. If you or your mate violated any of these three elements of safety in your relationship, what are some tangible steps you can take today to rebuild trust and safety?

TRUST

The confidence that one is true and authentic and can be depended on to carry out what they've stated they will or will not do.

I F YOU'VE EVER DONE STRETCHING EXERCISES, YOU KNOW IT CAN BE A good thing. They help make your muscles longer and leaner, improve posture and balance, and increase your flexibility. You probably learned that you don't stretch just once and call it quits—it's a consistent practice you commit to. We bet that you also learned not to overstretch (ouch!) and to work slowly to improve your reach and form.

Much like physical flexibility and limberness, relationship trust is earned over time through slow stretches, deliberate movements, and consistent actions. Trust, like flexibility, is not achieved in a day. It's developed as a byproduct of you and your partner's repeated stretching, bending, and flexing (consisting of actions, interactions, and behaviors) over time. And to continue with the stretching analogy, trust and flexibility are easier to build if no severe damage or tearing has occurred. It is far easier to build than to rebuild trust.

It's Not Just About Fidelity

When we ask our clients to share what mistrust or broken trust means to them, most immediately call out forms of mistrust related to cheating or addictive behavior(s). These certainly represent a significant breach of trust, but many couples will never have to navigate these serious breaches. And not every couple experiencing trust issues experiences a significant event or breakdown. Most of the time, relationship trust issues stem from a series of small, less severe events that erode trust over time. Things like not following through, dropping the ball at important times, minimizing things that are significant to a partner, and dismissing the feelings (including fears) that their partner has.

Have you ever seen the movie, *The Break-Up,* with Jennifer Aniston and Vince Vaughn? There's a scene where Aniston is preparing for a dinner party and wants to create a centerpiece with lemons, so she needs her boyfriend, Gary (played by Vaughn), to pick up twelve lemons. Instead, he comes home with three. When questioned about bringing home only three, he tells her to change her centerpiece, then dismisses the idea of the centerpiece she wanted to make, and, at one point, even tells her that the chicken dish could use those lemons instead. To some, this may seem like an insignificant exchange—it's just lemons, right? But, if we pull back the layers and look below the surface, we see one partner failing to follow through on a request, taking no responsibility for dropping the ball, and then minimizing the importance of what the other partner was trying to do. If this type of exchange happens regularly, it will erode trust in any relationship.

It's Not the Same Across the Board

It's worth noting that a trust issue in one area does not necessarily translate into another area. You may have great trust in your husband to be faithful and true to your vows, but that doesn't mean you trust him to wash your favorite dress or to take your three-year-old out dirt bike riding with his friends—not because he will purposefully do something wrong, but maybe because you just don't feel that he would place the same value you would on the issue. Or, perhaps, that task is just not what he's best at. Likewise, a husband may not feel comfortable with his wife driving his restored classic car to the store. The risk of dinged doors seems higher because she always parks up front in the narrow-

> Trust is more of a
> continual process
> of knowing your
> partner and being
> known by your
> partner.

er spots, while he always parks out on the back forty.

It's very common to trust more in some areas than others. However, a lack of trust in certain small areas can be a tell-tale sign of greater problems. Trust is more of a continual process of knowing your partner and being known by your partner. Trust (and likewise, mistrust) are built on knowledge, understanding, and awareness. You trust when you know your mate. When you know someone is being authentic, you see, feel, and trust them differently. That's how trust is established.

In this section, we want to establish and reinforce a better understanding of the power of trust and to look at the things we do (consciously and unconsciously) to erode or build up trust in a relationship.

If you have ever seen inside the cockpit of a large commercial airplane, you surely noticed all the dials, knobs, switches, and levers. It's overwhelming at first. But each one of them has a function. A seasoned pilot, through training and experience, has learned what each one does and is therefore not overwhelmed or intimidated by them, even though at one time, that pilot didn't know what they were all for. Trust is similar. Just as I don't expect a new pilot to immediately know what to do without practice, I understand that experience with your mate over time builds your knowledge and expectations. Trust is not something you start with—it's something you build. And for some, trust is something you need to rebuild. Rebuilding happens after trust between you and your mate has been broken. Rebuilding also needs to happen when trust was broken with someone else in a previous relationship and the mistrust has been carried over and applied to the new partner.

Rebuilding Takes Time

Trust is necessary to a healthy, thriving relationship. It is the foundation on which everything is built. If your relationship is one in which a significant betrayal has taken place or is taking place, it is completely understandable if you can't imagine ever trusting that person again. And while this may be how you feel right now, we can assure you that outside of a significant personality disorder or untreated addiction, most relationships (yes, most) can repair and rebuild from what you might have once thought was a dealbreaker, such as an affair. The first step is a commitment to rebuild.

You likely recall Hurricane Katrina that struck Louisiana in August of 2005. It was a devastating disaster. We recall the images from the news and the 1,800+ death toll. Millions displaced and cities destroyed. Fifteen years later, there are still ways in which they are rebuilding. A catastrophic natural disaster can bring years of recovery. Similarly, the bigger the blow to your trust, the more time it can take to rebuild it.

Understandably, it may be difficult to want to commit to rebuilding, whether for fear that the disaster will happen again or out of embarrassment of what others may think. This will be especially true if you're not the one who committed the act of betrayal. But even the person that committed the indiscretion, themselves, may struggle with trusting.

Despite the struggle, in most cases, it is worth it. We see most long-term damage to people's ability to trust stemming from previous relationships in which they suffered betrayal. They carried over that experience and applied it to their new relationships, rather than staying in the original relationship and working through the muck to understand and rebuild. We have personally witnessed countless couples in and outside of our practice who initially had little to no desire to mend their relationship, only to say later that the affair and recovery was "the worst best thing that's ever happened to their marriage!"

To be clear here, whether dealing with an affair or some other indiscretion, in the vast majority of cases, it's much easier (and wiser) to fix what's broken than to throw it away and start fresh. The caveat is that both (and it has to be both) parties are willing to fully engage in the process that will take their relationship to where it's never been before.

Not everyone is willing to do this. Likewise, not everyone should. The wound may seem too great. The fears are too strong. The betrayal is all they can see. The likelihood of recurrence is too great. But if they *are* willing to be authentic, transparent, and vulnerable with one another, despite how difficult that can be, they have an excellent chance of not only saving the relationship but rebuilding it and reestablishing mutual trust to better than it ever was before. Note that we didn't say it would be easy—just worth it.

Kelsey and Ben were married five years when Kelsey had an emotional affair with Randall. Kelsey and Ben decided to commit to counseling and rebuild their marriage and trust. Five years later, Ben had an affair with a coworker. However, this time, Ben wasn't willing to seek counseling or work to rebuild the marriage. He stated that he was afraid history would repeat itself in the future and that he didn't want either of them to go through this again. They ended up divorcing.

Sometimes It's the Small, Consistent Things

In relationships where both parties are truly authentic, transparent, and vulnerable with one another, people will fight long and hard to protect and save the relationship. People in those relationships rarely cheat, lie, or deceive their partner. They don't report having unmet needs (real or perceived) that lead to the breakdown in trust. These needs are addressed before they lead to an indiscretion. Unmet needs (known and unknown) are what cause people to seek something that they know will violate the trust of their partner.

Trust is established in lived-out experiences. If something is important to you and you've authentically disclosed this to your partner (not just what, but why), that thing should also be important to your partner. Recall the example from *The Break-Up* that we shared earlier in this chapter. The lemons were important to her, but he dismissed that.

Trust is not situational. Authentic trust says that even if you're not around and no one will find out, your needs are still important and honored. That's what establishes trust. People don't often understand the mechanisms, inputs, and subsystems that drive it—much like all of the buttons, knobs, and switches in the large commercial airplanes we mentioned earlier.

It is natural to want to be with someone who's trustworthy. What is unnatural is the willingness to see and understand the co-created process of how trust is built and eroded. We have never worked with a relationship with a severe breach of trust that didn't also experience smaller unrecognized or unresolved trust issues early on. Maybe the smaller erosions didn't look like big deals at the time. But we know that small doses lead to big results (in good and bad situations).

For years, Kevin has arrived home late for dinner. He calls each evening to tell his wife that he's left work and that he's heading home. But, almost inevitably, something stops him on the way and delays his arrival. His wife has learned over the years not to trust his "I'm on the way" calls and frequently distrusts his words about when he'll be anywhere.

Kerri has made a habit of overspending when she's out with her girlfriends. Although Kerri and her husband Tom have an agreed spending limit, Kerri very often blows the budget because, "It was a good deal," or "It was on sale." Now, Kerri and Tom find themselves at odds with one another before Kerri even leaves the house for outings with her friends. It's understandable that Tom finds it difficult to trust Kerri with money and finances.

Trust is Many Pieces

Trust is tethered to the other essentials of this book by understanding that they all work in concert together to move you toward your goal. Picture trust as an orchestra and the other elements of this book as the individual musical pieces that compose it. **B is for Belief** is the flute, **K is for Knowledge** is the trombone, etc.

Orchestrating trust is not simply seeing the world from your perspective, but also seeing your partner's perspective, too. It's not about demanding your way but seeking to understand why your mate may want it done differently (without just assuming they're wrong). It's about confronting conflict and working through your differences together, staying flexible enough to embrace the massive amount of change a couple faces in a lifetime. It's also not about tolerating bad behavior but rather maintaining an open line of effective communication. All of these are parts of trust, and when they're occurring, trust is found because trust is experienced.

Do You Trust with Your Heart?

When we talk about trust with clients, one of the questions we often ask is, "Do you trust your partner with your heart?" Most believe their partner is a trustworthy person, yet many also believe that they can't trust their partner with the most intimate details of their lives. They've either been betrayed by others before or they've perceived that their partner would judge them—or worse, exploit them or expose them to others. This is the core of trust, and it is the place where the deepest level of trust needs to be built.

The follow-up question to, "Do you trust your partner with your heart?" is, "Can your partner fully trust you with their heart?" People will adamantly exclaim, "Yes!" but further discussions typically reveal that this is less than true. If they're honest, they'll begrudgingly confess, "Well, maybe not fully."

The biggest issue that keeps people from entrusting others with their hearts is fear—fear born of previous hurts and wounds or fear of a potential breach in the future. But the lack of disclosing and attuning to one another within a relationship never lets you build (or rebuild) trust. It creates a *Catch-22* situation. Whether your fear is real or perceived, its impact is the same. "If I perceive that you'll tell your best friend something I'm struggling with, why would I feel safe telling you?"

Deep, intimate relationships grow from a willingness to see and witness your partner, including the thoughts, hopes, and fears that differ from yours. Think of it as the discovery of your mate. In discovery, the goal is to reveal—not to critique, judge, and evaluate. This is huge. Too often, our clients only listen to their mates to evaluate and correct them. There's more on this in the **Q is for Quieting** element. Your role is as yea-sayer, not critic.

Nothing shuts down communication faster than the belief that your partner is not listening or understanding but just waiting to pounce with criticism. Understand that different ideas, thoughts, approaches, and philosophies do not equal being "wrong". Newsflash: It is not your job to be your mate's critic unless they've invited you to be. And an invitation to brainstorm or critique one time is not an invitation for chronic, lifelong criticism. Commonly, we see couples who think that because they understand their partners, it is their job to point out to their partners how wrong or flawed their thinking, opinions, or approaches are. In those shared moments, whether consisting of delight, discovery, or oppression, trust either grows, stalls, or wilts.

The Bottom Line

When faced with conflict, relationships have the chance to either build back stronger or build a wall that separates them, sometimes permanently, undermining all chances of renewing trust. Most of the trust issues in a relationship aren't the "big" issues, but rather the result of thousands of small cuts that didn't get addressed. It's easy to get into the blame game of, "They should know," or "If they really cared, they would have known." Like so many of the other elements in this book, trust is a two-way street that starts with this: how trustworthy are you to hold your partner's heart?

If you have experienced a severe breach of trust, you may be wondering what to do next. Based on the depth of mistrust and damage caused, you may likely need the assistance of professional counseling. If this is you, you'll need more than this book. You'll need wise counsel to help you understand the dynamics of the co-created experience and to help you to walk out of the dark forest you're in.

A LOOK IN THE MIRROR

1. Have you and your mate ever experienced a major breach of trust? How did you rebuild?

2. What small acts of mistrust have you experienced in your current relationship? Were they resolved?

3. Do any current trust issues stem from your present relationship, or do they carry over from past relationships being applied to the present?

4. What do you think is the biggest contributor to trust in a relationship?

5. What are some ways that you and your mate have rebuilt trust or could rebuild it after a breach (whether small or major)?

6. Do you fully trust your mate with your heart? Why or why not?

7. Are you confident your mate could say they trust you with their heart? Why or why not?

UNDERSTANDING

A perception and knowledge of the significance, cause, character, and nature of something.

WE TRAVEL... A LOT! IT'S A PASSION FOR US. ADVENTURE AND travel and exploration. We love to see new places, meet new people, taste new foods, and expand our little world. But our trips would not be nearly as successful without the help of one of our favorite GPS apps. When we set out on each of our adventures, we know where we are starting and where we want to end up. But the GPS app we use has an insight that we don't have. It sees the big picture and every side road in between. It evaluates each road along the way and reroutes us as needed to avoid delays, traffic, and accidents. It gives us a heads-up if there's road construction along the highway or maybe even a police officer (of course, we're always cautious of obeying the speed limit). Our adventures are more of a delight because this smart phone app perceives problems, has knowledge of the road ahead we cannot yet see, and navigates us accordingly.

This is what understanding should do. Having understanding is to know life's patterns and seasons and let that knowledge help us navigate them—including the common ones to expect and the ones unique to you and your mate.

The idea of understanding is not just a simple awareness of facts, the ability to have clarity about your relationship, or knowledge of some unfolding event. It is much more. It's the understanding that goes beyond one's sense of present state to a greater understanding of life and the seasons and transitions a relationship goes through across the decades.

Memory is Fluid

Much like an often-traveled path, we tend to believe that life is somewhat static—that our path, interests, and concerns change little over time. One of the reasons for this is that the memory of our life events doesn't take into account the fact that as we grow and mature over time, the story of our story (the meaning that we give it) also changes. This impacts our ability to accurately remember details as experienced in the moment they occurred.

There have been several studies on this topic. One of them was a 10-year study of 9/11 survivors in New York City in the days following the events of September 11th, 2001. Researchers asked a group of survivors to describe where they were, what they saw, and how they felt about their 9/11 experiences. Ten years later, they gathered the same group and asked the same questions. The researchers were surprised to find that the majority of the participants had significant changes to their story. The biggest changes in their narrative were where they were and what they saw. The most shocking discovery was that the more convinced a survivor was of their story, the more likely it was to have significantly changed.

This research highlights the limits of and speaks to the fallibility of memories and the tendency to re-author our life's history. This is why Joel can look back forty plus years to the time he served on a nuclear submarine at the height of the Cold War and, for the most part, have nothing but fond memories. Of course, if it was that good, he would have stayed in the Navy longer. The point is that our memory of our memories changes as we all, to some degree, author and edit our life's story.

What does this have to do with understanding? Everything! Understanding is about coming to terms with how life's seasons will and do impact one's life and relationships. When we look at the seasons of one's life in association with an intimate partner, the only thing constant is change. Not just the seasons of life, but also the memories of those seasons. This explains why people will have such positive memories of a past relationship and yet forget the fine details that brought about its demise. It's common in counseling to have people get into the "Could have, would have, should have" dynamic that drives so many to Facebook and other social media platforms to look up past loves. This, sadly, has devastating results for many relationships when boredom, dysfunction, and resentment set in. It can lead people to start questioning current life situations. This is why having a good understanding of "Understanding" is so important.

In life and relationships, we'll often be forced to reconsider and question our choices and whether we've made the right ones. If we doubt our choices, we'll engage in second guessing and exploring our options. Understanding is being able to zoom out and recognize our various seasons and life transitions. It's being able to understand our tendency to glamorize and memorialize our past. It's understanding that we may not fully understand how many ways we'll remember the present as we struggle to understand the changes and challenges that lay in our future.

> Understanding is being able to zoom out and recognize our various seasons and life transitions.

Looking to the Future

We've talked about understanding as it relates to our past and how that affects our need to re-author history and reconsider our lives, but let's take a minute to look at the seasons and changes that so often affect our relationships across a lifetime. It's worth noting that people are often driven into couples' therapy because of one of the many life transitions. Couples can often navigate one season well but not others, and we've noted that people will most often seek counseling during one of those transitions.

What works at one point in your life may not work in another. And it is not unusual to hear a couple in counseling say "we were fine until".

In life, as well as in relationships, you're always in the process of redefining yourself as well as your relationship. The following are some of the most common areas we see couples struggle to traverse.

The Honeymoon Phase

The honeymoon phase is the first and often most dramatic change. In this season, you are moving from an individual to a couple. This is a season marked with many great moments along with several missteps as you work to move into becoming a couple. The future is wide open, and you're hoping to avoid the problems other couples experience, and you assure yourself that your life will not be like theirs. You have confidence you're not going to have "those" problems. As you move through this stage, you may be able to glide through without issue, but many people struggle to learn how to be a couple. This is often seen in those that have waited to marry later in life or who have been single for an extended period of time.

In our experience, this honeymoon season is the biggest struggle for people in their late 30s and 40s who've waited to get married. Learning how to become a "couple" and all that involves can be difficult if you don't understand the challenges and processes. Generally, most couples navigate these waters well, although the end of the honeymoon phase can leave some couples feeling that they are falling out of love. We contend that they don't fall out of love. Rather, these couples more than likely let their love wane because they stopped courting each other once they got married.

Early Career and Family Building

This phase is marked by the building of careers and family at the same time. As you work to find and build your collective family identity and establish what that will look like, old family traditions and customs will need to be adapted. This is also the time that you'll both work to build your careers and/or begin to have children. This often brings about questions and moments that cause you to reconsider what you want out of life and what's important to you. Some couples might become frustrated during this stage—wondering if they picked the right person and path for their lives. This period can be even more intense if the relationship didn't transition effectively during the honeymoon phase. You may want to see **J is for Joining**.

There are many common dynamics at play during this phase. Females will often go into "Mom Mode" with the birth of their children and the subsequent shift in life priorities. Husbands can become disenchanted with family life and the all-too-common lack of intimacy. Understandably, men may shift their interests from their wives to their work as a way of finding more meaning, purpose, and control. Their relationship may be struggling, but they take solace in focusing on building their career as a way to support their family, in an attempt to gain approval.

This is a time when sexual dissatisfaction can come to light at the same time external family issues start to emerge. The greatest need in this stage is for couples to find their own rhythm in life. They need to work to make their relationship a priority rather than a side note in a list of missed connections and disappointments. Otherwise, they may get distracted or lose focus as so many do in this stage of life. This is the period we see as the most vulnerable to affairs. Understanding these dynamics before they happen can help you avoid, minimize, or at least be aware of them so you're not caught by surprise. Like other seasons, this season comes with its fair share of conflict that will need to be worked through. Your ability to remain authentic, transparent, and vulnerable is important. Couples that navigate this season well are engaged, able to talk through their issues and needs, and deal well with conflict.

Empty Nester

Empty nesters are couples who no longer have children in the home. The empty nesters we typically see in our office have learned how to be great parents over being a good spouse. Out of all the relational issues, empty nesters are some of the most frustrated couples we see in the office. Often, they've become comfortable with being in parent mode and will sacrifice their relationship at the altar of being a good parent. While that sounds noble, the result is that they raise great kids at the peril of sacrificing a healthy and thriving marriage. Sadly, just as most couples are finally able to slow the hustle and bustle of life and parenting, they start to ask the question, "Who are we to each other?" Many of them have learned the dance of keeping up appearances for the sake of the kids and society, but once the kids are grown, they not only don't know their partners, but they question whether they even like them.

Strongly engaged couples will realize that they have a problem and take measures to rebrand their relationship. Couples that successfully navigate this stage can go on to have a happy and thriving relationship. By this time, most people have become more comfortable in their own skin and are able to find a path through the woods that saves their shared history and softens past failures as they work together to build a new life. This can also be a second honeymoon period where couples can finally spend time on their relationship and rebuild some of the bonding opportunities they sacrificed. These couples use gratitude over grumbling to reframe their shared life.

Retirement

Retirement is called the golden years, and for some it can be just that. For others, it can be a season met with bad health, missed opportunities, and painful memories of a lifetime of struggle or regret.

People in this stage seem to find themselves in one of two categories: (1) gratitude and contentment or (2) anger and bitterness. This is a mixed bag, as many will be dealing with elderly parents as well as the introduction of grandkids. It's a point where some may enjoy more financial stability while others are struggling to make ends meet. This is another time in which we see couples come into counseling because they are no longer working and are now spending more time together.

Many who find the golden years hard haven't really considered what they'll do with their life once they retire; and, based on our human condition, we don't do well when we lack meaning and purpose. This is a time when people will reflect on what they consider will be their life's legacy, pondering *"What did I do to show I was here?"* They become more interested in the past than the future. They can often spend a considerable amount of energy reliving past events and finding comfort in the life they knew rather than the world changing around them. You find them reminiscing about "the good old days" while new technology and change are met with a growing level of confusion, suspicion, resentment, and outright rejection.

However great your relationship can be, and no matter how well you've navigated the waters of life, each and every relationship comes to an end. Each one of us will someday say goodbye to our mate, and one of you will be left alone. While this may seem sad, it also should serve as the wake-up call to make each day count.

The Bottom Line

Understanding is about coming to terms with life and how short it really is. It's about learning to see our lives not by whether we got what we wanted out of it, but by whether we truly valued the time spent living it. It's about writing our stories and finding its meaning. It's looking at what we focus on to get our meaning and purpose. Our stories will either be focused on the good and grateful moments we had, or whatever we didn't get and all the people that did us wrong.

In our practice, we've had the honor to work with people who have graced this stage by inspiring others as they focus on a life well lived. We've also been privileged to work with those who have been stricken with regret and resentment. It's been said that your life is like a painting. You can paint paradise and walk into it, or you can paint hell and go there instead.

A LOOK IN THE MIRROR

1. What season of life would you consider yourself in right now?

2. What is your understanding of your current season and the one you're headed to next?

3. How does understanding the various seasons of life help you navigate them?

4. Do you ever find yourself with distorted memories of the past? In the "could have, would have, should haves?"

5. How have you and your mate been able to navigate previous and current life seasons?

6. In what ways do you feel that you and your mate may lack understanding and have room to grow?

7. What story are you writing for your marriage right now?

VULNERABILITY

—

*Uncertainty, risk, and susceptibility; the
quality or state of emotional exposure.*

To be honest, we're not big art aficionados. Don't get us
wrong—the creative genius of painters and sculptors fascinates
us—we just lack the knowledge to really appreciate the craft. But we
did read recently about the number of rare, famous paintings that many
museums don't put on display. And we found it a little mind-boggling.
Can you imagine something so unique and beautiful being kept hidden
for no one to appreciate? We know that a lot of it must have to do with
preservation—the fear of the art being harmed or damaged—right? But,
that fear of damage keeps those with immense appreciation for the work
from being able to view the creation and all its glory. And to us, that
seems like the real tragedy.

We know a lot of people who do this to themselves. They are so afraid
of experiencing harm and damage that they metaphorically lock themselves away.

Vulnerability is the willingness and ability to lay bare before another
through the authentic and transparent disclosure of one's inner self to
another in relational intimacy. It is the willingness to be fully seen for
who you are, warts and all, before another.

The Mother of All Fears

For many, the very idea of being fully vulnerable to their mate is a
frightening idea. Because of experiences with persons unworthy of trust

in the past, many people were judged, shamed, or rejected in some way (whether real or perceived), and learned to choose protection over participation to avoid being hurt again. This is such a common factor in the couples we've worked with that it's by far the most significant hindrance out of all the other elements we cover in this book. It's the #1 fear that keeps people from ever being able to connect at a deeper level.

True intimacy (and we're not talking sex) is deep interpersonal connection with another. It's the warm, fuzzy feeling we all long for in our relationships, and it can never happen without the willingness to be fully exposed and vulnerable to one another. It's like trying to swim without getting into the water; trying to bake a cake without turning on the oven; *or like trying to dance without any music* (okay, that can actually happen). Too many people enter relationships thinking that they can find safety and security without being truly vulnerable—or they want the other person to be vulnerable with them, hoping that will be enough. Sorry, but love just doesn't work that way. Love is scary, messy, and unpredictable, which is why so many are unwilling to be vulnerable with their mates. They are longing for certainty in something that's very uncertain and out of their control. If you're a person that longs for certainty and control, this chapter is for you—the price of admission to true intimacy is, in fact, vulnerability!

So, before we go any further on this topic, we need to acknowledge that there are often very good reasons to avoid being vulnerable with a person. If you're in a relationship where there are safety issues or any physical or emotional abuse, including active addictions or affairs, we don't recommend this without the help of professional intervention. Vulnerability requires safety, and if you're in a relationship that's not safe, you need to read **S is for Safety** before embarking on vulnerability.

Even if you don't have a current safety issue but have never been actively vulnerable before, we recommend you move into it slowly, with some caution, and in a controlled manner. One of the worst things you can do is overexpose yourself too early, be met with a perceived rejection, and be driven deeper into isolation building a wall of safety. That scenario can prevent you from ever finding true relational intimacy.

In-To-Me-See

When we think of the word 'Intimacy', it should be thought of as "In-To-Me-See". It's the method of looking into the heart and soul of another person. To pull it off correctly, it's the act of two people engaging with one another. Interestingly, humans are the only creatures that make love face to face, where we can look deeply into the eyes of the other person. The eyes are the gateway to the soul; and while many couples have sex, many can't gaze into one another's eyes while doing it. Sexual intercourse is the physical manifestation of what should be happening emotionally between mates—a part of one person is entering into another through the exchange of two lives. Lots of people are trying to find love in the act of sex; but sexual intimacy is the byproduct of the emotional intimacy that comes first. It's interesting: men will often give love to get sex, while women often give sex to get love. We then wonder why couples have such difficulty in the bedroom. First and foremost, it's really about a willingness to be emotionally vulnerable with one another at a deep and intimate level. Fix that, and the other aspects of your relationship seem to just fall into place!

So, how do we go about becoming more vulnerable? It's a process, and hopefully by now, you can see that most of these 26 essential elements dovetail into each other. You'll never be truly vulnerable if you don't have what is known as "felt security," a sense of relationship safety. What we're advocating is simply a willingness to see vulnerability not as a threat or something to be feared, but as a place you'll need to be "comfortable being uncomfortable exploring". It starts with finding out which areas you might need to work on in other elements of this book, such as trust, loyalty, and conflict. You may need to do that work before you jump into the deep end of vulnerability.

Ditch the Floaties

We like to use this analogy: To create vulnerability, both partners need to be willing to explore the shallow end of the pool before getting to the deep end. Maybe you can only put your feet into the water—like reading about this topic before trying to revolutionize your relationship; then wading around in the shallow end of the pool until you're comfortable there; then moving successively deeper into the water until it's up to your chest; and then getting you some floaties so you can paddle around in the deep end. The trick is that as you take each step, you gradually get more comfortable with the deeper levels. Before too long, you're in the deepest end and letting go of the side of the pool. You've not only learned the skill of floating, but you also know that you're never too far from the side of the pool if you need to swim to it. You've learned to trust the safety and security of becoming vulnerable together. For many couples, exploring one another and becoming comfortable with the feeling of being uncomfortable is a lifelong process.

Sadly, most people have never seen a truly vulnerable relationship modeled in their own family of origin. Too many people had families that were either in extreme conflict (where every feeling was broadcast for all to witness no matter what the setting) or extreme avoidance (not allowing any conflict at all and stuffing their feelings, rarely resolving anything). Neither of these models are effective ways to foster "felt security;" nor do they create a place of acceptance and safety that enables you to understand when "This person is safe to be vulnerable with".

Vulnerability is a combination of becoming aware of your internal, emotional world and being willing and able to express it to your partner in a way that reveals your intentions. In other words, is not merely good enough for your partner to hear the words you say. Understanding the authentic message you are trying to express is the ultimate goal. We have a saying that goes something like this: "You don't have to agree with somebody to understand them; and understanding them doesn't mean you necessarily agree with them."

Understanding vs. Agreement

Too many people think that understanding our partners' point of view on a matter means that somehow, they are giving up ground or are saying that their partner is right and thus they must wrong. Nothing could be further from the truth. You give up nothing in the process of understanding your mate. We can tell you after seeing hundreds of couples that the number one complaint we hear is, "My partner just doesn't understand me!"

Here's another issue that limits vulnerability. When people feel that their partner sees things differently it can cause some to become deregulated and lapse into "You always," or "You never" statements. When your partner doesn't see things the way you do don't fall into the trap of trying to correct with facts. Instead, be willing to seek the meaning of the underlying issues.

Too often, we listen only to prepare a response instead of listening to truly understand the other person. Vulnerability is about accepting and celebrating each other's differences, learning not just what they think and feel, but going deeper and understanding why. Vulnerability is not only your willingness to be explored, but to make your thinking more visible to your partner in the process.

There's another significant pattern that prevents most people from the willingness to be vulnerable. It's believing that they already know what their partner thinks and therefore they jump to conclusions and make broad, sweeping, and incorrect assumptions about their partners motives and feelings. These false beliefs are often based on incomplete information, hunches, or underlying facts and meanings that aren't fully understood.

It's Not About the Fork

There's a story that I, Joel, often tell my clients. It's about a couple I helped years ago that came in for counseling after a 35-year-long marriage. Now, you should understand that most couples coming in generally have long lists of complaints and failed attempts to resolve their differences. However, this couple was different. When I asked them, "What brings you to counseling?" Sharron, the wife said, "You know, things are pretty good between us; we just have one small problem..."

"Just one?" I waited to hear what it was. She started talking about how after dinner each night, she cleans up the kitchen, and later, Jerry, the husband, comes in and makes himself a snack.

Sharron continued, "Inevitably, when he's done, he'll leave the fork in the sink, and it drives me nuts!" She went on to say that she's asked him for years to put the fork in the dishwasher, but he never does. "In fact," she continued, "if he keeps doing it, I'm going to divorce him!"

My eyes widened as the word "divorce" floated throughout the room. I then asked, "So, if we get this fork issue resolved, everything is good?" She responded with an emphatic "Yes!"

I then said, "Sharron, I'm going to go out on a limb here, but I bet you've got more things wrong with this marriage than just that fork; because if everything was really good, Jerry could put every fork you own in the sink, and it would not have that effect on you. You might not like it, but it wouldn't be the sort of thing that would cause you to consider ending a 35-year-long marriage."

So, what does the fork in the sink story have to do with vulnerability? Everything!

Sharron's lack of vulnerability kept her from making her feelings and thinking visible to Jerry. Sure, she told him a million times that she didn't like it, but she never told him what that fork in the sink meant to her. So, I asked her, "What do you feel emotionally when he refuses to put the fork in the dishwasher? What story do you tell yourself about that fork?"

"It tells me that he not only doesn't care, but he does it to hurt me!"

Jerry was surprised and responded, "It's just a fork. How do you get that out of a fork?"

Sharron had never told Jerry that as a little girl and the eldest sibling, her job was to clean the kitchen. Every night, her father would come home, and if anything was left out, he'd wake her up and tell her to correct it. Her father's love, she learned, was conditional, and there was no grace. She was only worthy of love if things were done a certain way. She associated Jerry's unwillingness to put the fork in the dishwasher as meaning, that she was never going to be worthy of love—leaving her to feel that she was never going to be good enough.

Jerry was floored and deeply troubled. "Why didn't you ever tell me that story?" he said. "I just thought you were bitching at me."

When questioned about what he felt, Jerry said that he just felt disrespected. "What difference does it make if the fork's in the sink or the dishwasher? It's still dirty."

Neither of them ever expressed the deeper meaning of what they were feeling. Sure, they talked about what they didn't like. Sharron told him countless times to put the fork in the damn dishwasher, and Jerry, feeling controlled and manipulated, was being passive-aggressive in responding to what he thought were unreasonable demands.

The moral of this story is that vulnerability is the key to unlocking the deeper meanings of what we feel and why we feel it. It's the gateway to discovery and attuning to one another. Neither of them wanted to hurt the other, but neither ever stopped to look below the surface for a deeper awareness of where they were. Vulnerability is the vehicle that transports a relationship from the surface, or shallow end, to the deeper, In-To-Me-See side of the countless issues couples face.

Lack of vulnerability keep some couples from resolving even the simplest of conflicts, let alone any of the complex issues.

Lack of vulnerability keep some couples from resolving even the simplest of conflicts, let alone any of the complex issues.

The Bottom Line

Vulnerability is about developing the willingness and skills to make your thinking visible and creating a safe place to enable your partner to feel secure enough to be vulnerable with you. Women often report that their men are void of emotions, but we've learned over the years that men are far more sensitive to criticism than rumored. Too often, men feel that they can't let their feelings be known because they'll be accused of being wrong or weak. It doesn't matter if that's true or not—if it's perceived by either of you, it will nearly always limit your chances of vulnerably and relational intimacy. Thus, keeping you stuck in the shallow end of the relationship pool.

A LOOK IN THE MIRROR

1. Who in your life is a good example of how to practice healthy vulnerability?

2. How would you rate your ability to be vulnerable with your partner?

3. Who is more comfortable being vulnerable—you or your mate?

4. Do you equate being vulnerable with being weak?

5. Do you have a "fork in the sink" story that you have never shared with your partner?

6. What is one thing you can do this week to make your thinking more visible to your mate?

7. What is your biggest hurdle to being more vulnerable with your mate?

WISE COUNSEL

Getting the best advice. Only the wise can give it and only the wise will listen and receive it.

A S YOU CAN LIKELY TELL BY NOW, WE LOVE THE CINEMA. MOVIES are exciting and engaging, and we enjoy looking for underlying themes about human nature and relationships in the movies we watch. When we started writing this element, we knew exactly what movies we would reference. We're curious to know if you initially think of the same characters.

Yoda. Wise is he. (See what we did there? HA! Please don't close the book on us!) As the legendary Jedi Master of the *Star Wars* series, Yoda counsels leading man Luke Skywalker in his Jedi journey against Darth Vader's army. How about Albus Dumbledore? Remember him? He's the headmaster of Hogwarts in the *Harry Potter* series who counsels and protects young Harry Potter. Mysterious at times, he seems to always have a way of guiding Potter and his friends out of trouble. Or maybe you think of Miss Clara in *War Room,* who teaches the leading lady (played by Priscilla Shirer) how to fight (in her closet, on her knees, in prayer) for her husband and her marriage.

Unlike the other elements in our **A-Z** approach to wildly successful marriages, we've intentionally given this one two words. This is important. We all have a plethora of counsel available to us: some good, some bad, and some indifferent. But, for a thriving marriage, it's *wise* counsel we are seeking.

Is it Wise?

Counsel comes in many forms and from a variety of sources. We can get advice from friends, family, influencers, clergy, etc.—solicited and unsolicited. Things we read (like this book), listen to, and witness could qualify as counsel. Counsel even includes social media "friends" weighing in on relationship topics and so much more. Today, we are drowning in information but dying for a lack of wisdom. Everybody has an opinion, but few seem to have any real wisdom. This chapter isn't about just *any* sort of counsel related to successful marriages. This is about "wise" counsel and how to differentiate and accept wise counsel rather than counsel that may be ineffective; or worse, harmful (eek!).

To gauge if someone or something is wise counsel, consider these three things:

First, let's acknowledge that it's human nature to look at things from only our point of view (or at least from a narrow point of view). This means that a situation is filtered through our individual hopes, dreams, fears, ideas, beliefs, and experiences. We don't intend to be narrowly focused or biased—it's just human nature. Being aware of this can go a long way toward offsetting it.

Second, it's natural to want to garner support for a journey or struggle; win people over to your own side; gain empathy and support; or even triangulate to relieve anxiety.

Triangulating means that we bring in others to get support for our side, like rallying the troops. An angry wife might call up her mom or sister to complain and share just enough of the story to get their support. A husband may resort to enlisting his single buddy who thinks "all women are crazy" and hence is a lifelong bachelor. We innately know whom to call when it's a pat on the back from a "yes man" (or woman) we're seeking.

In therapy and mentoring, we warn clients not to triangulate or bring others into the situation just to tilt the scales in your favor. The Beatles'

With a Little Help from My Friends is a great song, but sometimes in relationships, it muddies the waters and can even compound problems. [BTW, we like the Joe Cocker version of the song better.]

We've noticed a destructive new twist on triangulation. People have taken to social media to win others over to their side. Social media allows you to triangulate with people you don't even know, compounding the problem because you don't know their biases or history before they give you their two cents. Maybe they are thrice divorced, a man or woman hater, or widowed. These anonymous social media "friends" (yes, we used quotations for a reason) don't know the history of the problem, don't have the ability to see the whole picture, and don't understand the nuances that each couple brings to a problem. Further, what are their credentials? Do they have the experience to help get to the root of the issue and ask the questions that ferret out those deeper issues? Do they ask the tough questions that get you honest answers? We're guessing not.

Third, at one time or another, we all need wise counsel related to relationships. Please recognize that it isn't weak to need or rely on wise counsel for difficult or unfamiliar situations. Rather, it's an incredibly brave, strong, and—catch this—wise thing to do. Think of wise counsel like a guide or Sherpa. No one would think about climbing Mount Everest without a Sherpa or hiking the entire Appalachian or Pacific Crest Trail without a map. That would just be unwise. But there's a unique skill to recognize and rebut counsel that is unwise. And it's rare for us to see our own weaknesses and needs.

Wise counsel comes in a myriad of shapes, sizes, and forms, including resources that encourage and support what is best for you overall. Wise counsel are people who know and believe in you. They are people who believe in marriage in general. And also believe in *your* marriage. They are the people who can put aside their own agendas, bias, and history to help you sort through what is best for you. These are the people in your life who will ask you the tough questions and encourage you to take a

360-degree look at challenges in your marriage—meaning not just looking across at your mate, but looking all the way back at yourself, too!

Wise Counsel May Not Come from Close Friends or Family

Friendships are important for an overall full life. They bring joy, laughter, and oh-so-cherished memories. A good friend will be loyal to you (as they should be) but therefore not necessarily a good source for the best advice. They may be the best friend, but not necessarily the wisest counsel.

Do you remember the movie *This Means War* with Reese Witherspoon and Chris Pine? In the movie, Chelsea Handler plays the leading lady's friend, Trish, who lives vicariously through her friend, giving unrealistic advice based on her own internal struggles. We all know a Trish. We love her and appreciate her loyalty, but she's not our wise counsel.

A good friend is going to want to come alongside you and support you in troubled times. When you hurt, they hurt. Their loyalty, however, can inhibit their ability to see the big picture and limit their ability to give you wise counsel.

When you want counsel, you need someone that will take in the full picture, not a narrow section of the picture.

Decades ago, a friend of mine (Kimberly's) was struggling in her marriage, and several of her friends told her to leave her husband. They told her that he would never change and that he was too domineering. One of these friends was widowed. One was divorced. One friend had never married. And then, there was me. They all said she should leave him, and I was the only friend to encourage her to hold on, slow down, and consider how she had invested 13 years into this marriage and two kids. Fast forward in time—she didn't leave him. They recently just celebrated their youngest kid graduating from college! She now says that it was tough and required a lot of hard work, but she is glad she didn't follow the other friends' advice to leave.

Our family members, friends, fellow MOPS, (Mothers of Preschoolers) or car club pals may not be our best sources for wise counsel. If you're badmouthing your mate because you're upset, a loyal friend will side with you and hold it against your mate long after you've repaired the situation. After all, commiseration and misery do not just love company but demand it. A good friend does not want to see you hurt and will want to keep you from harm, so be sure to update them on the repair to the marriage. That will help prevent their loyalty to you from poisoning your relationship well.

We often confabulate and do not give a fully detailed and accurate account of situations—or at the very least, our account is one-sided. This results in your friends relying on their love for you and certain inaccuracies or omissions (or worse) that they gather from you to give you good, sound advice. They rarely have the totality of the facts, and their best interpretation of the situation will be skewed.

Wise Counsel May Not Come from Church Friends

Sadly, some people's fellow parishioners can also be harmful to a marriage. Their theological twist can poke holes in your marriage—sometimes by encouraging couples to sweep problems under the carpet rather than resolving—and sometimes by insisting you stay married at any and all costs.

Wise Counsel Rarely Comes from Social Media

Wise counsel does not come from those anonymous social media "friends" mentioned earlier. (And there we go purposefully using quotations again.) In several social media groups that I (Kimberly) belong to, I see desperate, frustrated, troubled people reaching out for advice from others—people they do not know. They tell their story about how they're upset with their mates about this or that and how he or she is horrible because of this or that. In some cases, the concern seems legit. But often-times, the situation that was shared is not that unusual, and they're just unwittingly looking for a place to vent their frustrations. What they are sometimes looking for (and often find) is support from other people that keeps them from having to admit their own contribution to their marital problems. Sometimes, they are honestly seeking good advice, but others chiming in add fuel to the fire without fully understanding the dynamics.

It is rare that we see a social media advice-giver asking follow-up questions to better understand or challenge the original poster. How many marriages have been undermined because of cavalier or flippant social media advice given by people who are not equipped to give it?

Consider this recent Facebook post:

> *My husband wants me to be a stay-at-home mom, and I want to go back to work part-time. I try to bring it up, and he just won't listen.*

And here's the bad advice that followed:

> *I would threaten to leave to show him you mean business.*
> *This is abuse, you need to leave him now!*

There is little to no discussion from the social media advice-givers. No one is asking: Is the conflict about your financial well-being or personal values? Do you need the money, or is it more of an existential search for something such as being more than a mom right now? How much will daycare cost? What agreement did you both make about being a stay-at-home mom?

The authentic problem is often so much more complicated than what it seems to be on the surface. And it's likely that the person telling the story doesn't really understand all the facets of the situation they're de-scribing. Or, if they do, they would rarely be willing to share it fully.

Another Facebook post I saw recently was by a woman whose husband apparently wouldn't give her carte blanche access to their bank account. Social media folks give this flippant advice:

"F*** him."
"I would leave him if he said that to me."
"You will be fine on your own, you don't need him."
"You will be better off without him."
"He doesn't appreciate you. This is abuse."

The post could have easily been written by a number of our clients who only focus on a snippet of the story as if that were the whole story.

I (Kimberly) had a client that had a spending problem and got upset because her husband controlled the money in the marriage. But what she did not voluntarily share is that she had driven them to the verge of bankruptcy TWICE due to her secret overspending and gambling habits. And, they had both agreed that it was best for him to control the money for a while.

Another social media poster asked in a Christian Wives group about what to do when she caught her husband looking at porn. Most of the advice given by the group participants was actually destructive, not helpful.

Remember: the empathetic ear that you run to is not the one living your life, nor will they have to live with the consequences of their advice.

A Therapist Might Not Be Wise Counsel

Unfortunately, sometimes therapists are no better. If you're in individual therapy, your counselor is likely getting only one side or a skewed version of the story. A therapist wants to believe you, support you, and build rapport with you, but it takes an exceptional therapist to dig deeper to get to a fuller picture. We like to ask our clients questions like: *"What would your partner say if they were sitting here? How would they explain the situation? And what would their view of your interpretation be?*

Therapists have the greatest intentions, but they can be led astray by their desire to be helpful. And their perceptions of your situation can be filtered through their own life experiences, and so they may be triggered or not see things for what they really are. And that doesn't include the therapists that have their own agendas. This may be unsettling or surprising, but some therapists are biased.

A therapist in our area was once "taken in" by a boyfriend she believes was a narcissist. Now, she often diagnoses husbands as narcissistic, without even meeting or properly assessing them. This is unprofessional and disturbing. If you are working with a therapist and they diagnose your mate as a narcissist without meeting or properly accessing them, I (still Kimberly) am concerned for you and the therapist's ability to be effective for you. You and your therapist need to be honest and remember that they are only getting one side of the story. Making an assessment on this limited perspective is unprofessional.

Our best results come from meeting couples together and then meeting separately to hear their take without their partner's comments, etc. We get to see if they describe their problems differently or if they can be more open.

Also, consider your counselor's history. What are their beliefs? Are they looking to find abuse, trauma, attachment injuries, or repressed memories (buzzwords that get thrown around, but might not actually apply)?

The often-undervalued power of therapy, however, is that sharing your story or troubles with friends, family members, and co-workers can change the relationships you have with them; but talking to a therapist about your situation *shouldn't*. Therapy is an opportunity to freely talk and explore your thoughts without the potential judgment you might get from friends and family. Additionally, one of the added benefits of therapy, that you might not get from others, is confidentiality.

Wise in Some Ways & Not in Others

Interestingly, what makes one person or source wise counsel in one area does not make that person or source wise counsel in another area. There are different people who are wise counsel in different areas of life. It's important to identify who and when certain people are good or bad sources for advice. Seeking marital advice from a friend who is divorced or single may not be balanced. Marital advice from your financial planner may not produce good advice, either. Think about getting advice on raising your kids from someone without kids. Laughable, right?

The Bottom Line

Now that we've eliminated those who are NOT likely to be your source for wise counsel, we hope your gears are turning. We hope you're thinking through all the people you know that may fit the criteria for wise counsel—the person(s) who will ask the tough questions, dive deeper into the complete story, challenge you, support your marriage (and not just you), and encourage what's best for your marriage. Remember, what's best for your marriage is ultimately what's best for you, too. Of course, if you're not safe, your safety is always a priority, and we recognize that not all marriages can be or should be saved.

> Listen for the voice of wise counsel and filter out the rest.

We also hope that you now understand the difference between counsel and wise counsel. You'll always be inundated with lots of voices from friends, family, social media followers, fellow parishioners, and perhaps even a therapist. Listen for the voice of wise counsel and filter out the rest. Remember, being "right" isn't necessary for a healthy, thriving, successful marriage. But, seeking and following wise counsel is.

A LOOK IN THE MIRROR

1. In what areas of life am I wise counsel for others?

2. What are the vital qualities that make wise counsel for my marriage?

3. Who is the best wise counsel in my sphere?

4. What experience or education makes them wise counsel?

5. Who in my sphere would **NOT** be wise counsel for my marriage?

6. Who do I think would be wise counsel to my mate?

7. Who would I prefer them to **NOT** seek counsel from?

X-FACTOR

The willingness and desire to have an active form of physical intimacy between you and your partner.

WE CANNOT WRITE A BOOK ABOUT MARRIAGE AND NOT INCLUDE the most controversial, intriguing, mysterious, stimulating, curious, pleasurable, powerful, historical, desirable, exciting, maybe even scandalous topic of all! So, here it is, finally we're talking about S-E-X! It's about time, and if you're reading this, we can't help but wonder, what was the first letter you turned to in this book? Was it "S"? If so, we hid it! The sex talk is here in X for X-rated!

When it comes to sex, there is no such thing as "normal". That's just a setting on the dryer. We've worked with both individuals and couples, and if there's one thing, we can assure you of, most couples are not having mind-blowing sex each and every time. In fact, most couples are often not balanced in the area of physical intimacy. So, if you're having some intimacy differences, you are probably more "normal" than you think. Most—if not all—couples struggle at one time or another with their physical intimacy.

It Really Comes Down to One Thing

There is no sexual benchmark for frequency, duration, and activities. Neither medical study nor sex therapist can dictate what normal or even a great sexual relationship should look like for you. There are definitely several factors that play into it, but it really boils down to just one thing:

Is it healthy for both of you?

When it comes to physical intimacy within a relationship, we would say that there's really only healthy and unhealthy. That is worth repeating. Not normal and abnormal. Just healthy and unhealthy.

Over the years it's been rather eye-opening to see just how complex of a problem physical intimacy can be for some couples. What's even more interesting is the lack of ability most couples have in authentically talking about this subject—let alone agreeing in practice. In fact, we can count on one hand the number of couples we've talked with that had a great sex life but a bad marriage. A couple's physical intimacy is probably the best single indicator of the quality of one's marriage. Some may not be engaging in much sexual intercourse but still report having an active and satisfying sex life. This is often the case in couples with some physical limitation or other limiting factors.

> A couple's physical intimacy is probably the best single indicator of the quality of one's marriage.

When it comes to numbers, as a general rule, if you are having less than two shared sexual experiences per month, you are in what is often considered a sexless relationship. However, we've had couples that are both fine with that, and we are in no way saying that's not right for them. Likewise, we've had clients on the other end that report engaging in sexual intercourse daily. Most physically healthy and attuning couples would fall somewhere around 2-3 times a week, but will also say they have spells where they may go a week or two between being intimate. Again, it's not about what you do or how many times you do it, it's really about healthy and unhealthy expressions of physical intimacy that we want to cover or, should we say, uncover in this chapter (see what we did there).

Don't Get Bored

There are thousands of "How To" books lining the shelves on how to have better sex. Some are good, some are okay, and others are concerning. We take the position that anything two committed adults engage in that is not forced or demanded is probably okay. Trust on this, there are countless ways people fly their freak flags, but we're not going to explore those here other than to say that in a healthy, loving relationship, a couple should never get bored with sex.

Sexual intimacy is yours to enjoy (yes...ENJOY!) and your marital relationship is the place to explore it. For both of you. Many people (we would venture to say almost all people) enter their marriage with pre-existing ideas of what's allowed and now allowed (see **B is for Beliefs**). These ideas may be influenced by what their families taught them, religious backgrounds, or what culture has deemed as acceptable. Your marital bed should be the safe place to explore your curiosity, passions, your body, and your mate's body—even if someone else would label it racy or even kinky. However, the key word here is "safe" and safe means that *both* mates are willing to agree and want to freely participate.

Most intimacy issues within a relationship come down to two problems: 1) a lack of emotional intimacy in which one or both feels unloved, unsafe, or disrespected or 2) a crisis or lack of engaging their sexual imagination. Sexuality is really the playground of a couple's relationship. Your partner is the only person (or should be) that you take your clothes off with and do the things you do together. To keep things fresh and alive, it takes some effort and imagination to feel safe enough to explore one another. Sadly, many individuals have been victims of abuse—whether physical, sexual, emotional, and yes, even cultural. For many, any sexual expression was considered wrong, dirty, or even sinful. We can't tell you the number of young couples we've worked with that can't mutually have an erotic identity of their own because they consider it sinful. Seems silly, but we often have to remind people, God created sex to be enjoyable, and you don't need to pray beforehand!

Healthy sexual expression is anything the two of you do which you both feel safe and are emotionally engaged in. You may engage in an activity that may not blow your hair back, but for the sake of the relationship, your partner may find it very enjoyable. There are a lot of things we do for our partners that may not be our cup of tea yet means a great deal to them. What would make you think sex would be any different? If it's something you find morally offensive, or you feel pressured to do, or it's painful (and we're not talking the good kind of pain—wink wink), you shouldn't do it unless it's better understood, talked through, or changed in some way to be "healthy." Anything that falls outside of that is unhealthy by definition.

When Things Are Cold

So, what if you have a partner that can, but doesn't want to have sex or engage or be a part in some shared sexual identity? The first question is, have they ever been? If the answer is yes, but they aren't now, what's happened? Has there been a significant breach trust? Were they pressured into something they didn't want to do and now have associated sexual intimacy with fear and pressure? Or have they always been uninterested? The answers to these questions lead us down different paths for solutions.

In our experience, we find that where the marriage relationship goes, so does the sex. Meaning, when couples are emotionally and mentally in tune with one another, they are physically, too. When you feel distant from your mate, the sexual drive isn't exactly leading the way. Take make-up sex for example. You and your mate have just had this major disagreement. But you work to understand one another, hash through the issues, come to some sort of compromise, and then WHAM! You're having mind-blowing and passionate make-up sex. You were separated by your disagreement, but your communication and reconnection brought about a physical reunion, too.

If you and your mate are in a funk or a sexual freeze, the issue may not be the sex at all. More times than not, it's a mental or emotional or even spiritual issue. Before jumping to attack your mate for their lack of sexual initiation lately, take a look at what's going on in their life. Are they stressed? Are they hurt? Are the two of you struggling emotionally? Do you have some other unresolved conflict? If there are lingering issues, your mate may not feel safe to be sexually vulnerable and adventurous right now. Find the source of the issue and work to resolve it, and the sexual reconnection will typically follow. Again, it's about healthy and unhealthy. Resolving conflict so it doesn't negatively impact your sex life is a healthy approach to intimacy.

Human sexuality is one of the most complex dynamics of our humanity. Nothing is more convoluted and mysterious than what turns us on and off sexually. The issue for many couples is that they are so stuck in their heads (whether over or under engaged) that they haven't built a relationship of open and authentic communication to work through and unwind the complex relationship that each has with sex, let alone be able to engage or come to some meeting of the minds. Many are just too scared or embarrassed to talk about it, so they spend years not getting their sexual needs met in a healthy way.

One of the biggest issues we see in our practices is the growing number of relationships that have to deal with porn and/or the countless ways in which individuals seek connection outside of their relationship. Whatever kind of sexual act you may be interested in; you can find it within a minute or two on the Internet using just your smart phone. It's pretty hard to pass up the substitute in light of whatever reason (perceived or real) you think your partner doesn't accept or want to be with you. Porn is a formidable foe. It will almost always win.

We can debate the morality of porn, but the thing you can't debate is the damage it does in wiring and rewiring the brain. Porn acts to soothe and give immediate gratification, rather than having to put in the emotional effort to stay engaged in a real relationship. Over time, porn has been shown to kill the ability to be authentic and transparent, generally because the partner who's indulging in porn knows their mate disapproves and the resulting outcome is often shame, guilt, and a mate that's more detached emotionally. This further causes division in the relationship and a feeling of rejection, thereby starting and perpetuating a cycle that leads to addiction and compulsive behavior.

It's Not Just a Man's Struggle

While this has often been an issue which men face, there is a growing number of women who are joining the ranks. This is no longer only a man's issue. Besides, too many women are engaged in romance novels and Hallmark movies to the point where they have an unrealistic view of intimacy that leaves them comparing their partner to someone who isn't real, and they can never live up to. Women complain, and rightly so, that they can never compete with airbrushed porn, especially after birthing a couple of babies. Likewise, no man can ever compete with Noah Calhoun from the movie *The Notebook!*

Don't Be Too Shy to Ask for Help

No woman wants to feel she's being used sexually and that she's nothing more than a sexual object to her husband. Likewise, no husband wants to be given pity sex and know that his wife isn't into him or enjoying their time together. This is a complex problem that again, requires legitimate intimacy to work through. Sadly, too many couples fail to either work through issues or get the help they need. Sometimes, based on past traumas, people may need to do some individual work to see what stories they believe about themselves and to come to terms with their own sexuality. We've seen women who are so turned off by sex that they have prayed their husband would develop erectile dysfunction (ED), so they won't be expected to have sex with them. Even worse, we've seen wives offer to pay for their husbands to visit a prostitute. This isn't a healthy view of sex. These issues aren't resolved through shaming, and we're not meaning to single out wives. There are plenty of husbands that for many reasons struggle to perform and meet the physical needs of their wives.

There are countless resources out there for couples struggling in this area. Ideally, counseling can help you unpack and work through your issues. The goal is to understand your individual erotic identities and to create and recreate one as a couple. It's one thing if you can't engage in sexual activity with your partner, and it's another if you won't.

It's Never a Weapon

A final and necessary area to address is the people who use sex as a weapon and lord it over their mate in an unhealthy way. Too often we see couples that engage in this sort of destructive and abusive behavior. No person should ever be pressured to have sex, and no partner should be lorded over or manipulated in order to get their physical needs met. That is not acceptable and it's extremely unhealthy.

Further, rejecting your mate sexually as "punishment" is not a healthy way to resolve a conflict. In fact, it only multiplies the problems. Instead of having one hurt to work out, you've added another to it. Sex is not a treat to dangle over your mate's head so you can train them like Pavlov's dogs.

Is it possible that a person is unwilling to have sex after experiencing some kind of hurt from their mate? Yes. And this goes back to the emotional connection we talked about earlier. Resolve the emotional and mental disconnect and let the physical connection fall into place.

The Bottom Line

The X-Factor subject has been covered by endless books on countless bookshelves, so we're not going to try and cover it all here. The point we'd like to leave you with is that in order to have a wildly successful marriage, you need to also have a successful X-Factor in your marriage, which requires you to have a safe and solid emotional relationship. Regardless of how hard it may be, you owe it to yourself and your mate, along with the relational example you set for your kids, to have them see you engage in appropriate physical intimacy. You are helping to develop your children's views of sex. Maybe you can give them what you never got!

A LOOK IN THE MIRROR

1. How would you describe your sex life right now? Hot, cold, or lukewarm?

2. Do you think your mate is satisfied in your intimate life right now?

3. What active role do you play in creating physical intimacy with your mate?

4. Do you have any unresolved past hurts or traumas that are negatively affecting your physical intimacy?

5. How comfortable do you and your mate feel discussing sex with one another?

6. What are your preexisting beliefs that impact your sexual intimacy?

7. What is are some ways you can help create a safe space to grow your physical intimacy?

YEA-SAYER

One who has an attitude of confident affirmation, belief in, and support.

HAVE YOU EVER FLOWN ON A PLANE FOR A LONG DISTANCE? ACROSS the country or maybe overseas? Years ago, we took a once-in-a-lifetime trip to the Mediterranean. It was a long trip from the West Coast to Rome, but well worth it. We had a wonderful time.

But we noticed that the return flight was longer than the flight out!

It was the same trip. Same airline. Same path. Same plane, actually! But coming back took an extra two hours. Do you know why? It's because our flight to Italy had the tailwind to help us, but the wind was against us on the way back! The journey home took longer because the plane faced the resistance of the headwind.

Similarly, marriages face a smoother ride, mates meet their goals more easily, and both spouses have an easier time pursuing their dreams when they're supported and encouraged by a "tailwind" of support from their mates. In contrast, the journey to our dreams and goals is a lot tougher when our mates are "headwinds" of opposition, objections, and cynicism.

When we are yea-sayers, we're offering tailwinds.

Yea vs. Nay

A yea-sayer is optimistic, hopeful, and helpful. They are believers, visionaries, and dreamers. They see new opportunities as a chance to learn, grow, explore, and live! They cheer on others. They encourage others to push forward, to say "yes," to go for it, and to live out that famous slogan of "Just Do It!"

Naysayers are the opposite. They discourage. They are skeptical, pessimistic, and cynical. They dissuade others from trying new things, and they crush dreams. They focus on what can go wrong, refuse new opportunities, and live life as a bit of a sourpuss feeding on fear. Their headwinds can be so strong that they slow—or even halt—their mate's progress.

Yea-sayers aren't just "yes" men/women who tell us what we want to hear. They instead cheer us on, support us, and push us toward our dreams. Yea-sayers are optimistic and pleasant to be around—and wonderful to be married to. They are a tailwind. Naysayers live life like Eeyore and are often rather unenjoyable to be around—and yes, at times unpleasant to be married to.

Grab the Pom Poms

Our job in our marriages is to help our mates be all they can be, and their job is to do the same for us. We are to see the very best in our mates; not just who they are but who they can be, and then lift them up as they work toward that. Our mates should be our biggest supporter and we should be theirs. The loudest cheerleader. The one that roots the longest and hardest. The one who rallies the troops on our behalf. The truest of all friendships.

> A yea-sayer will tell you to give your dreams a try—even if it doesn't work out.

Yea-sayers have an attitude of investment. They believe in their mate as an investment—not a simple case of Pollyanna or looking through rose-colored glasses. Yeasaying is grounded in reality but also looks at and believes in the possibilities of who your mate is capable of being and what they are capable of accomplishing. A yea-sayer will tell you to give your dreams a try—even if it doesn't work out. The journey of trying is important, and so is having a mate who believes in you. Yea-sayers know that to discourage you because you might struggle or fail is to clip your wings before you ever had a chance to fly.

Being a yea-sayer is being the holder and dispenser of optimism and hope when your mate is low or unsure. Your job is to help your mate dream bigger, to brainstorm, and to rally the possibilities. You get to help your mate be all they can be.

Yea-sayers are there to help bail when water starts coming in. They are there to hold the ladder, throw you a pulley rope, or go get help when you're in a difficult situation. Instead of sitting back saying, "I told you so," they show loyalty in action and practice by jumping into the mess with you and helping you fight the rising flood waters.

Dreams Come True with Yea-sayers

Are you helping to make your mate's dreams come true? Do you have a couple's bucket list? We do.

Sometimes what is overall best for the relationship is whatever is best for your mate and their dreams, and not necessarily for you (at the moment). Reread that last sentence and let it sink in. When you got married, you became part of a team. Two became one. And the well-being of the marriage became more important than your individual desires. However, there are times when your mate's dreams and best interests ARE what's best for your marriage overall. In the best relationships, partners will give and take, and each will have turns at having their wants, dreams, and desires come true. Thus, the relationship will flourish, and the individuals will as well.

Remember **O is for Opportunity**. There is tremendous opportunity in each partner saying "Yea!" to the other's goals and dreams.

The Devil's Advocate

Sometimes naysayers mask themselves by playing devil's advocate. When their mates approach them with a new idea or desire, they immediately start calculating what could go wrong. They may have good intentions in trying to ward against the worst-case scenarios or thinking they are protecting their mates from making bad decisions.

But playing devil's advocate can be destructive. It doesn't always save you from bad decisions. In fact, it will often keep you from making any decisions, taking a leap of faith, or pursuing new ideas at all. It can gradually turn into a "nothing is going to work anyway" mindset.

On the contrary, the yea-sayer will find ten reasons why you *should* try something and will help you realistically drown out the voice of the devil's advocate. They help you work for solutions rather than devise all the reasons "why not".

Yea-saying Can Look Different

We would be remiss if we didn't acknowledge that yeasaying doesn't mean the same thing to everyone. Take stock of why.

Ania was frustrated with her husband because she felt he was being unsupportive. When probed, Ania revealed what support looks like to her and why she thinks her husband, Trello, was being unsupportive. We had her recall a time when he was unsupportive and a time when he was supportive. It turned out that Ania has a history of stopping and starting side jobs and activities ranging from Amway to a real estate license she never got, and more. Trello had lately become "unsupportive," whereas a couple of years previously, he was very supportive. This doesn't mean that he was being a naysayer. Instead, he had set limits, which is not an unsupportive stance. He had asked her to pick one thing and follow through with it.

Carli has an annual weekend trip with four high school friends coming up, and John is usually supportive and works around the annual girls' weekend schedule. But this year, the weekend falls during the launch of a huge computer upgrade project at his workplace. Because of this, Carli needs to either cut the weekend short or see if they can move the girls' weekend to a different date. Carli's friends were miffed when they heard about this, but Carli stood up for John, and said that he's always been supportive of the girls' weekend, and pointed out that there happened to be a conflict this year. Maybe the "naysayer" seems unsupportive because they are busy with other things, but sometimes, timing is everything.

Are They Really Being a Naysayer

What do you think naysaying actually looks like? Is it actively undermining and sabotaging? Is it being neutral or unengaged? Is it a temporary lack of support, as in Carli's and John's case? Understanding your own perceptions in recognizing and identifying naysaying can help to understand the kind of yeasaying you are looking for. In fact, if you really want to understand your mate and how they best support you, review the **K is for Knowledge** element to get a better feel of your mate's natural tendencies.

It's important to define and understand what kind of support you are looking for. Is it moral, emotional, financial, or intellectual? Does it involve the use of resources? Or is the type of yeasaying you want undetermined? Maybe you want your mate to pick up the slack on a project because you're overwhelmed, short on time, or feel underqualified. (Hands raised—who hasn't done that?)

Based on your and your mate's individual skill set, personal history, level of confidence in each other, the particular project, or the needs of the task, you might desire or expect yeasaying (support) in very different forms.

Could supporting and yeasaying mean that your partner just runs with a project and lets you get out of the way? Perhaps, but your partner might not know that you'd like that kind of support. Some partners would love to help but have a fear of doing it wrong or don't want to interfere. They might think that being your biggest yea-sayer means to encourage you while you struggle so you discover that you can do it. Your project may remind your partner unpleasantly of their own unresolved or unachieved goals. Or perhaps they are just oblivious to what is needed. If neither of you knows what would be most supportive, your chances of getting the yeasaying you need are diminished.

We assign meaning into actions or inactions that may or may not always be accurate. So don't assume that your interpretation is accurate.

Samantha was dating a guy, and she wanted to stop dating him because once, after dinner on his way out, he didn't offer to take out her trash can, which was full. When I (Kimberly) asked her if she asked him to take it out, she said, "Nope. He should have just known." She was testing him. "I wanted to know if he just knew to do things."

I, on the other hand, am more concerned with how he would have responded to a request rather than just expecting him to "know" things. That tells me more about the quality of the person.

People often expect mates to automatically know things without actually telling them. Is the yeasaying that you need clearly identified by form, level, time, degree, etc.? Our mates don't have crystal balls, so we can't treat them as mind readers. Rather than assume, like Samantha, just ask.

Uncertainty can lead a partner into becoming a naysayer. They may believe in you, but if they're feeling fear or uncertainty, they can project that onto a situation. They may be unable to be your yea-sayer because they feel unqualified on a given topic. They may not only feel a need to protect you when you're dreaming big but to protect themselves as well, making them feel too overwhelmed to meet your need for yeasaying in the moment.

You may get caught in this trap at times, too. Do you ever become a naysayer when projecting your fears onto the goals and dreams of others?

It is unreasonable to expect unfettered, constant, and full support at all times. Are you giving this to your mate 24/7? It's a great goal, but an impossibility. You may have to prioritize the times when you need support the most and request it at those times.

When people actively dissuade you from your goals, it feels like naysaying. From a wider view, you might see that those people are meaning to help you. Are they trying to protect you from harm? Address their fears and concerns. Review their backgrounds. Are they qualified enough on the topic to be naysaying, critical, or dubious about your approach? Could this naysaying be helpful because it's causing you to look at your goal from many different angles?

The Bottom Line

Our mates don't need another source of criticism or opposition in their lives. The world offers enough of that. Instead, we get to sit in a role with our mate that is unique, honored, and valued. We get to sit in the role of their biggest supporter. When we play the yea-sayer—as opposed to the naysayer—with our mates, we help bring out their best.

To support our mates and to best feel supported, we must communicate our expectations and desires. We cannot assume they will just figure it out. We also must avoid being a naysayer with our mates by projecting our own fears and insecurities onto them. We get to help encourage them to chase their dreams and then cheer them on and celebrate them as they do. What a privilege and a responsibility to be the voice of optimism to our mates!

We're not saying one should blindly support our mates in dangerous or harmful endeavors. Yeasaying has to be balanced against reality. Remember how we said that what looks like naysaying can actually be helpful? When your concern is clearly expressed out of love and support rather than mistrust and doubt, your mate will realize that you're yeasaying them as a person, even when you're cautious about supporting an idea that doesn't seem right.

We've seen some sad cases in which one mate gave the go-ahead and encouraged their mate, only to later criticize and blame when things went wrong. Sincere communication takes effort. Pretending to support someone and relishing failure (or even ridiculing success as a silly goal) is not yeasaying but manipulating. Instead of having honest conversations about latent hostility, the mate who finds it hard to be supportive just goes along and waits for revenge when their mate fails.

If your mate has lofty goals and you don't, you might feel small or inferior. Further, if you've got underlying problems in the marriage that aren't being addressed, or if you're secretly wishing to end it, you most likely cannot yeasay sincerely. For your sake and the sake of your mate, we wish you both a yea-sayer by your side.

A LOOK IN THE MIRROR

1. Do you brainstorm and daydream with your mate?

2. Would your mate describe you as more of a yea-sayer or naysayer?

3. Would you describe your mate as more of a yea-sayer or naysayer?

4. What is one way you can adapt your responses to your mate's ideas so that you are more of a yea-sayer than a naysayer?

5. Can you name one bucket list item or goal your mate has that you can help bring into reality?

6. Think of a time your mate has been your biggest cheerleader. What did it look like and how can you show gratitude for that?

7. Is there a time that you thought your mate was being a naysayer, but later realized they were being a yea-sayer?

ZEBRAESQUE

—

*No two zebras have the same stripes, and
no two marriages are exactly the same.
Be wildly different.*

SOME KIDS ARE REALLY INTO TRAINS OR DINOSAURS OR PRINCESSES or planets. When our kids were little, one of them was really into zebras, so we researched and learned a lot about zebras (seriously, a LOT of facts about zebras stored in our memory banks). One very interesting thing we learned was that all zebras are different—meaning that each zebra has its own unique pattern of stripes. How cool is that?!?

> A successful marriage is one that has enthusiasm for whatever makes your marriage unique.

Much like you and I have one-of-a-kind fingerprints unique to us, individual zebras have stripes original to them.

Marriages are wildly different, too. We call it the Zebra Effect. A successful marriage is one that has enthusiasm for whatever makes your marriage unique. It celebrates its one-of-a-kind "stripe" pattern instead of trying to look like other marriages. Long-lasting marriages avoid the harmful trap of comparison and find new ways to make traditions and customs their very own.

Ditch the Preconceptions and Comparisons

Understandably, most people have a preconceived idea of what marriage is, will be, or should look like. Perhaps your ideas stem from watching your parents, exposure to Biblical teachings, movies you saw, or cultural influences. Likely, it is a mixture of some or all of these. Too often, these preconceived ideas of what a partner and/or a marriage should look like limit people from truly appreciating what is unique about their own relationship. And honestly, it often plays out as a form of rigidity—causing us to show less flexibility, grace, and forgiveness for our mates and ourselves. It creates a cookie cutter expectation that all too often results in disappointment.

It is common—and honestly, a part of human nature—to compare ourselves and our marriages to others. But comparison hurts relationships and can be the demise of what could have been a happy, thriving marriage.

I (Kimberly) have always loved this quote from Theodore Roosevelt: "Comparison is the thief of joy." This is profoundly true! When we're busy looking around at others and rating ourselves against their marriages, someone must lose. Either we think our lives are better and we have it more together than other couples (creating a harmful sense of superiority and pride), or we think someone else is doing better—causing us to look down on ourselves, our mates, and eventually view our marriages as inadequate. Where's the joy in that? It leads to a discontented, "grass is greener on the other side" perception, which in turn lends itself to bitterness, affairs, disappointment, and potentially divorce.

If you want to compare anything, compare your marriage to where it was last year. Then ask yourself how you've grown or how your relationship with your mate has changed. If it's for the better, celebrate that! If it's strained, take the necessary actions (yep, it takes doing something about it) to get it back on track!

Do you buy into the whole "white picket fence" idea? Do you believe others have some grand, picture-perfect marriage just because it looks that way from the outside? Break free from that belief. Nothing and no one is perfect.

Social Media and Hollywood Set the Bar High (or Low)

Social media makes comparing easier and even more destructive. How many times do you scroll through your feed and see other couples smiling, hugging, and living it up, and you start to wonder why you and your mate don't seem to have that? Social media and all its filters (literal and figurative) create the opportunity for others to highlight only their best. They show you the family vacation—not the screaming match they had in the car on the way there. They let you see the completed home projects—not the foreclosure they faced on their last home. You hit "like" on their well-groomed, shirt tucked in, hair combed, smiling, happy family photo, but they didn't show you the miscarriages, negative pregnancy tests, and seemingly endless tears that it took to get there.

When you thumb past a post on social media that tempts you to compare your marriage to someone else's, remind yourself that you are seeing only the filtered best. Just hit "like" (or don't) and keep on scrolling. Better yet, get off social media, go find your mate, and give them a hug or kiss. That small act of love and kindness will move you toward a better marriage while comparing to others will not.

A well-known author and her motivational speaker husband have a huge social media presence. They had been seemingly happily married for nearly 20 years and recently announced to their followers how their marriage had been falling apart behind the scenes. Using them (or other celeb couples) as your altar and example sets you up for failure. You will start to believe that if they can't do it, neither can you.

Tinsel town and Hollywood are some of the worst examples of marital bliss to follow. Don't do it. However, we are impressed with Tom Hanks and Rita Wilson's marriage. We'd love to interview them some day.

In many ways, the Zebra philosophy of marriage is the anti-comparison philosophy. Learn from others, sure—just don't make the mistake of equating their journey with yours.

For example, it might help to look at what other people are doing well and consider the tools and resources they have. Maybe you can adapt or imitate patterns or techniques to improve your marriage, but don't seek to be like someone else. Remember: you and your mate are each unique with your own striped pattern. You two are unlike any other two people ever, so when you come together you will also make a relationship unlike any other couple ever.

Find What Works for Your Marriage

Uniqueness is—by its very definition—different from everyone else. In counseling, helping couples find their uniqueness is a goal. Rather than the "norm" (there we go with the quotation marks again), we strive not to compare or be rigid. And for the love of Pete, not to judge. We need to find what is unique about you as a couple and what makes you stronger and better because of it!

You have to find what works for you and your mate. Some marriages might be more female-led and others more male-led. They both work fine. Some couples report that without date nights, they melt down, while other couples are homebodies—perfectly content staying home.

Some are highly involved in their community or church. Some do yard work together as a date night and play in the backyard. Some couples are into board games. (Bunco night on Friday?) Some lay in bed at night and read books. Others binge watch television shows together. (Netflix anyone?) Some couples' lives revolve around their dogs/pets— and that's okay! Some have two houses instead of one.

We personally love to travel together—it's really important to us. We have routine, scheduled family night dinners every Monday and like to have getaways in a cabin in the woods on weekends. Friends of ours, Pam and Dan, love to go to wineries and pubs and play the ukulele and sing. A younger couple we know are the little league couple—mom brings the game snacks and dad is the coach. The possibilities are endless as the combination of couples.

Make Your Own Zebraesque Customs and Traditions

Wondering how your marriage can be more unique and fabulous? Look for ways to blend in or adapt traditions, rites of passage, or your own culture. Holidays and practices surrounding life events will help you feel more connected. As families become more spread across the world and busier, these traditions, practices, and customs are important to creating and keeping a sense of belonging and feelings of connection.

I (Kimberly) love my brainstorming sessions with clients looking to create or adapt family traditions. And, as time goes by, their traditions will continue to evolve. Here are some traditions former clients implemented in their marriages and other ideas to help you and your mate spark your own ideas.

Christmas Traditions

The Locke family owns a great deal of acreage. The year they got married, they planted a variety (based on species and rate of growth) of 25 "Christmas" trees, and an additional 25 trees each year that their four children were born. They did this in a special area on their land, and these trees were meant to serve as their family's private Christmas tree lot. Each year, they go as a family to pick their "family" tree. The adult children come to get their family tree each year now too. Another family would not have the knowledge, space, or the desire to do something like this. This is unique to the Locke family and something they get to enjoy every Christmas. It's a part of this family's Zebra philosophy.

Birthday Traditions

Every family does birthdays differently. One mom friend throws a giant celebration for each birthday. No gifts, just parties. And she goes all out with a unique theme each year. She takes lots of photos and fills an album with the memories they made instead of filling a toy chest with more garage sale fodder. Another couple we know (that share the same birth month) take a trip somewhere new to celebrate their birthdays.

Each family is different and even when you do the same things, you will do it in your own unique way. Take birthday pinatas, for example. Some families don't do pinatas; some make homemade pinatas; some people say "no hitting"; others pull strings; some use a bat but only use non-person-shaped pinatas; some put in candy only; some include trinkets; some people collect candy and divide it up for the children; and other people let the kids scramble for the candy in a Snickers/Skittles/Smarties free for all. Whatever your "thing" is, do it and enjoy it!

Thanksgiving Traditions

We saw a meme last Thanksgiving that joked about how everyone was eating the exact same turkey meal—based on the photos—so get off social media and go have seconds! While it made us chuckle and we support the idea of being present with family, we considered all the different traditions people were participating in across the country (or world) on Thanksgiving.

Some couples have a traditional Thanksgiving Day meal, while others (like us and our crew) have a traditional Thanksgiving meal a week later on a non-traditional day. Some make it a tradition to donate their time and energies to feed others at local homeless shelters. Some actually avoid Thanksgiving altogether due to bad family memories. Some excitedly watch the Macy's Thanksgiving Day Parade or go Black Friday shopping. And some don't celebrate at all: all very different and all very okay to do!

Rites of Passage & Other Special Traditions

Some families have special traditions for rites of passage or anniversaries. I (Kimberly) once read that author Bob Goff celebrated a milestone birthday with his kids by letting them pick any place in the world they wanted to go to, and then they went there. While most of us can't afford to do that, we can be creative and design special celebrations.

Another family I know took each of their kids to Washington, D.C. after each graduated high school. Each kid knew when their own trip was coming up and had time to dream and plan what they wanted to see and do. And each kid's trip looked totally unique and different from that of their siblings.

Some couples celebrate milestone anniversaries by visiting the place they honeymooned or by renewing their vows. Some rewatch their wedding video or look through photos. Some do nothing but stay home and enjoy a meal together. All great ideas and all very fitting to the couples who do them!

New Year's Word of the Year

Some couples come up with a Word of the Year to set a goal or theme for the coming year. This can be a fun experience involving all the family members or something simply between you and your spouse, but it can also be a way to help you focus on the qualities or goals you'd like to develop in the coming year.

The Bottom Line

Every marriage is different—as they should be. Find what makes yours unique and celebrate it. Zebras don't look at other zebras' stripes and wonder why their stripes are different or wish they looked the same. Instead, they run wild and free. Be "Zebraesque!" Avoid comparing your marriage to others because you don't know what's really happening behind that "white picket fence" mirage. Make your own traditions, your own memories, and your own special kind of love.

A LOOK IN THE MIRROR

1. What is the one thing that makes you uniquely suited for your mate?

2. What is the one thing about your mate that makes him/her uniquely suited for you?

3. What are three ways your marriage is different from others?

4. When was the last time you compared your marriage to someone else's? How did that impact the way you looked at your own marriage or treated your mate?

5. How does social media pull you into the comparison mindset?

6. What is one unique custom or tradition you and your mate have?

7. What is one tradition you'd like to implement in your home?

—

Your level of relationship happiness is directly dependent on your level of engagement, effort, and service to each other and your relationship. It is not a competition, unless of course you are both trying to out-serve each other.

—

FINAL THOUGHTS

___

So, now that you've read through all the elements, you may be wondering "What's Next?" Here's some final thoughts we'd like to share with you that we believe are important.

Every couple has their ups and downs. Each couple goes through easy and difficult seasons. Each person in the relationship brings strengths and weaknesses, and all this makes you normal. You are human, and we humans are a perfectly imperfect lot. Embrace it. And maybe even try to enjoy it.

As you reflect on the chapters in *Words to Love By*, know that from time to time you may want to revisit a chapter or you may find a chapter relevant that never seemed relevant before.

We have invested considerable time and energy, as well as our hearts into this book in the hope that we can reach more couples. Our goal is to help more people have stronger relationships and (optimistically) to make a dent in the divorce rates while we do it. We sincerely, from the depths of our hearts, want to help couples create their own unique and wildly successful marriages.

Here are our closing thoughts on how to create your own wildly successful marriage.

Love and marriage are best lived without a cookie-cutter approach.

Yours is not a prefabricated love, but more like a custom home built to your specifications that you remodel regularly as you go. The happiest marriages are made of two unique people coming together and creating something unique and beautiful together.

Be intentional.
Your efforts, actions, thoughts, words, and even your approach to love and marriage should be thoughtful and intentional. And your choices and actions should reflect your intentions.

Try different, not harder.
Don't try harder to improve your relationship—try differently.
Too often couples are stuck in unhealthy or destructive patterns. Doing more of the same thing, repeatedly using an unproductive approach that equates to hammering a square peg into a round hole, may be exactly what causes or worsens a rift between two people.

Don't wait to get help.
Our sessions are filled with couples dealing with years of hurts and disappointments behind them. If these were only addressed sooner, they could have served as stepping stones, not stumbling blocks. Don't wait to get help if your relationship is struggling. Find a therapist sooner rather than later. We consider EFT (Emotionally Focused Therapy) the most effective couples' modality. It promotes and encourages attuning with your mate; and wildly successful marriages begin there. You can find a counselor here: https://members.iceeft.com/member-search.php

Stop being easily offended.
Marriages are made of two imperfect people that are going to disappoint each other. Yes, it will happen. Focus on how to mend and repair rather than looking for reasons to be offended. Too many couples allow their emotions to be controlled by their partners. You need to own your emotions and stop blaming your feelings on your partner.

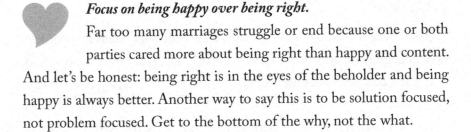

Focus on being happy over being right.

Far too many marriages struggle or end because one or both parties cared more about being right than happy and content. And let's be honest: being right is in the eyes of the beholder and being happy is always better. Another way to say this is to be solution focused, not problem focused. Get to the bottom of the why, not the what.

Embrace being perfectly imperfect.

Your mate is imperfect. You are imperfect. But that doesn't mean you're not perfect for each other. We like to say, "perfectly imperfect."

One person can change the dynamic.

If we could leave you with just one thought, it would be that while you can't force your partner to change, great progress can often come about from one person making slow and intentional course corrections. Over time, your mate will most likely respond to your course correction and begin to change so that you both reap the benefits. It may seem unfair if you have to carry more of the burden in the relationship—but the burden often does fall on the stronger partner. Again, this doesn't mean you should tolerate bad or abusive behavior. For some, maybe the best course correction is in setting better limits, while for others, it would be to be more flexible.

In Closing

Your level of relationship happiness is directly dependent on your level of engagement, effort, and service to each other and your relationship. It is not a competition, unless of course you are both trying to out-serve each other.

We know that love and marriage isn't as easy as the ABCs. Or maybe, perhaps, this book proves that love CAN be as easy as ABC when you know how to assemble the letters in the right order for you and your mate.

ABOUT THE AUTHORS

KIMBERLY WALTON M.A AND JOEL WALTON, M.A, WORK TOGETHER in separate, yet complementary, capacities in the marriage and personal growth fields. Joel is a Licensed Marriage and Family Therapist and Kimberly is a marriage mentor, speaker, and retreat leader. They are in private practice in Northern California.

Kimberly and Joel have diverse backgrounds and unique life experiences that give them a broad range of real-world experiences to draw from in order to serve their clients.

Kimberly has the heart of an educator and inspirer, and has worked as a radio personality, facilitator, trainer, and adjunct university professor. She is a lifelong student of customs, traditions, and rites of passage and draws on her formal and informal education including her own divorce to mentor her clients.

Joel has served on a nuclear submarine, as a reserve deputy sheriff, and as a volunteer firefighter. He authored five patents while working in private industry and served as a staff counselor for a large ministry in Roseville, California, before going into private practice. Joel has a second Master's in Biblical Counseling.

Kimberly and Joel are also bloggers, podcast guests, speakers/presenters, and lead small groups in addition to their private practices. They also work collaboratively offering weekend intensives for struggling couples wanting to save their marriages. If you'd like to work with Kimberly or Joel, please reach out at the below contact information.

CONTACT INFORMATION

Both Kimberly and Joel are available for mentoring
and counseling, as well as interviews and podcasts,
guest speaking, and small groups. They can be contacted
via their respective websites.

KIMBERLY WALTON, M.A.
www.cherishedwives.com

JOEL D. WALTON, M.A.
www.mendedlife.com